What You See Is What I Saw

Lessons for the beginning photographer

And presenting a sampling of

The Artistic Photography of

Tomas Howe

Preface

I began taking photographs in my late teens, inspired by my father, though an amateur, took wonderful pictures. To him it was a hobby, a delightful pastime even though he did take classes at the local community college and had many published in the Travel section of the San Diego Union.

He past the knowledge on to me and I began shooting with a 35 millimeter camera, teaching myself patience to capture the right photo at the right time. After all, film wasn't cheap for a college student to just plow through shot after shot like so many digital photographers do today. So when I switched to digital photography, I had already trained myself to shoot the best picture and not just a series of pics.

In this book, I present the beginner with ideas of what to shoot and how to shoot it. Also, all subjects are with natural lighting as studio photography under artificial lighting provides another skill level to alleviate artificial shadows or a "white out" effect.

I'm still picky as to what I shoot, or even whom I'll shoot. For it can't just have the potential of being commercially successful, but I must derive some sort of mental and emotional satisfaction that this is a photograph worthy of posterity.

The photos within designed as examples but are also available for sale on the websites at the end of the book.

A lot of my photography has garnished awards of which I'm proud of though I don't shoot for accolades or to become wealthy; for the wealth is in the satisfaction of a great photo.

Also, I must add that none of my photos have been manipulated by a "Photoshop" program.

Table of Contents

SO...

You want to be a photographer?

You've taken a few good shots and family members have said that "they're as good as anything else on the market," and you believed them. You've signed up for the photography class at your local community college and bought an inexpensive camera with multiple lenses at your local pawn shop and think you're ready to enter the competitive world of commercial photography.

Now a decision needs to be made: What type of photography do you want to specialize in? Not that you need to; but I have found that a photographer who tries to be good at many styles, is good at none of them. For landscape photography is quite different from portraits as skateboarding is from surfing. Yes, they both have similar aspects, but portraits require a studio and specialized lighting while landscapes, seascapes, sunsets require patience and a keen eye; though working with people requires patience as well.

I have worked with many genres and decided that working with nature gives me the greatest pleasure and the greatest opportunity to travel. So take a look at the pros and cons and how much the cost will be to get started. Remember your overhead costs for a studio, lighting, lenses, etc. as well as the cost of printing, matting and framing.

You may want to start a photo book with samples of your work where potential customers can pick and choose the photo size along with matting and framing options.

Don't forget, this is a business, so you will need a business name, business license(s) from the cities you plan to sell in and tax revenue retail sales license from the state you're in.

And you thought it was just going to be point and shoot?

35 mm

A Lesson In Patience

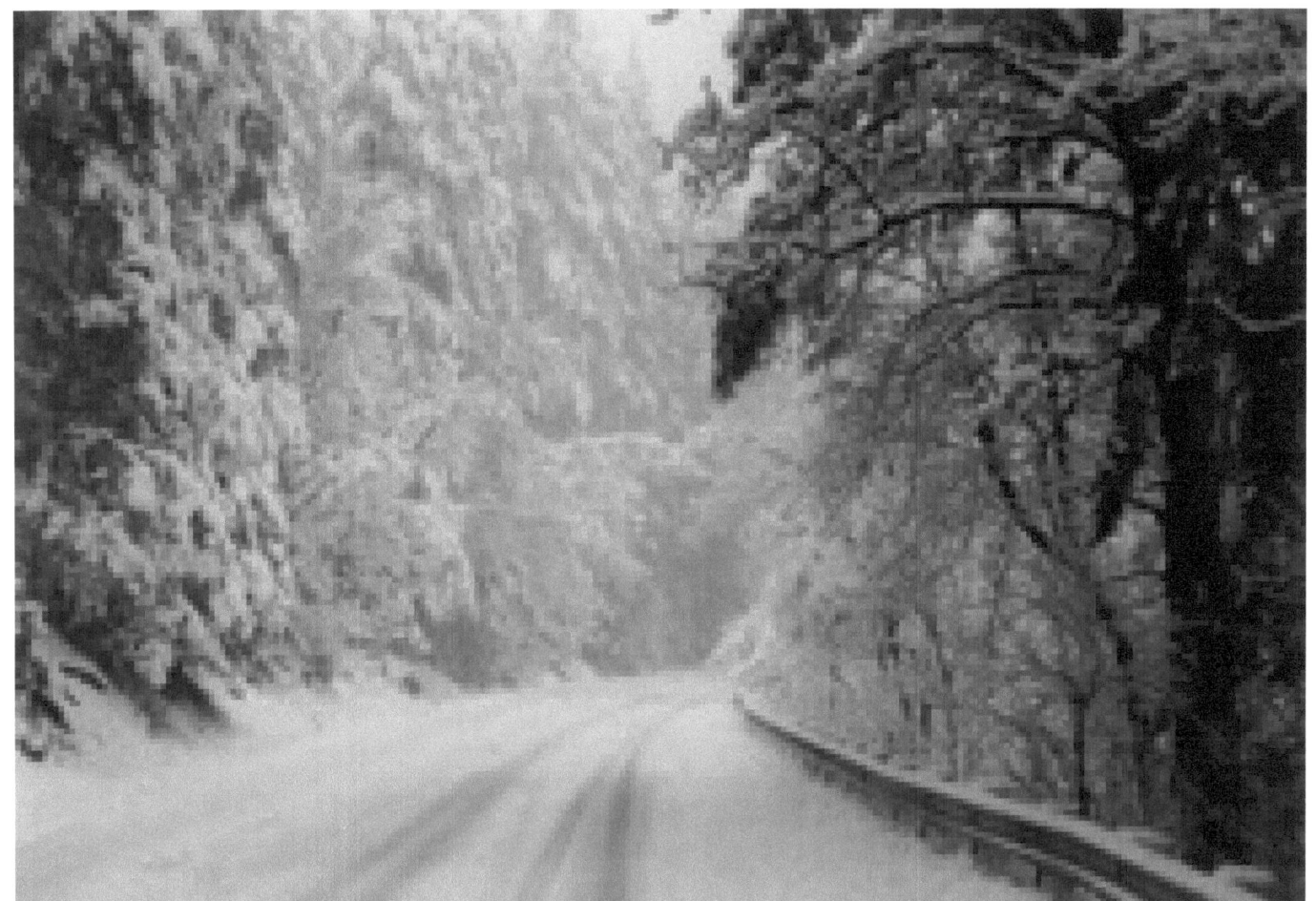

Oak Creek Canyon, AZ   April 1984

Deciding to visit the Grand Canyon during Spring break, we packed our SUV and headed out across Hwy 50 and down I-5, across the Mojave Desert and up to Flagstaff where we spent the night. We were greeted in the morning by a freak snowstorm and while others were busy digging their cars out of the motel parking lot, I put ours in 4WD and headed out toward Sedona via Oak Creek Canyon.

As we started down the canyon we encountered the beauty of the early spring storm on the trees and road. Clearly it was a winter wonderland. I only had back and white film in my camera, but after seeing this shot, was glad I did.

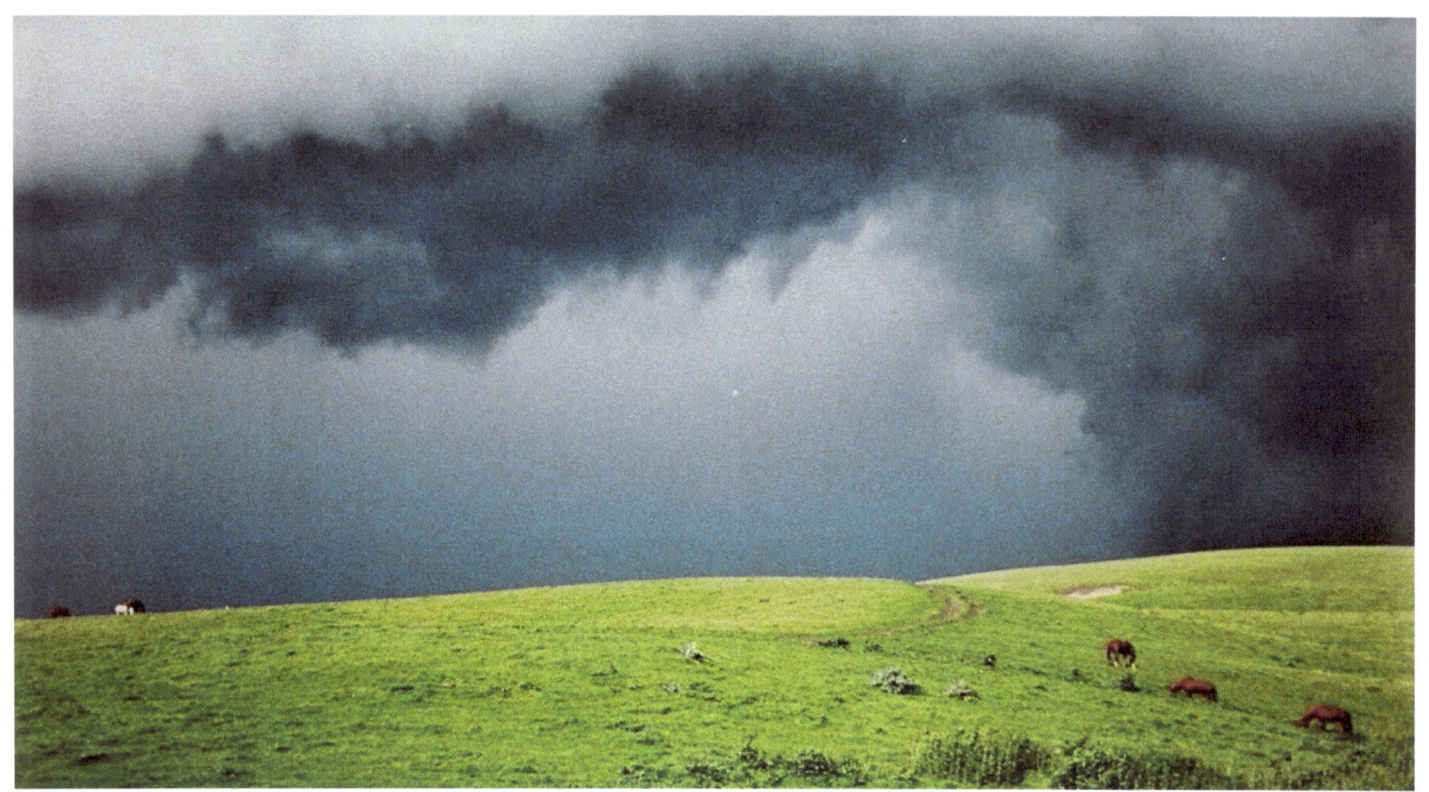

North San Jose, CA   October 1988

I worked as a school teacher in the North San Jose, CA area for a number of years and as a fledgling photographer had come to carry my camera around all the time in case the one in a million shot came along. It did...

Driving home from work one afternoon, I spotted this unexpected contrast between sun and storm with horses grazing on a green hillside. Needless to say, I quickly stopped, grabbed my camera and took this shot on the first try. With 35 mil, there is no wasting film.

While camping in Kings Canyon National Park in California, this sunset presented itself with the clouds creating this amazing color. I waited as long as I could and decided that this was going to be the best shot available. It was and still amazes people today.

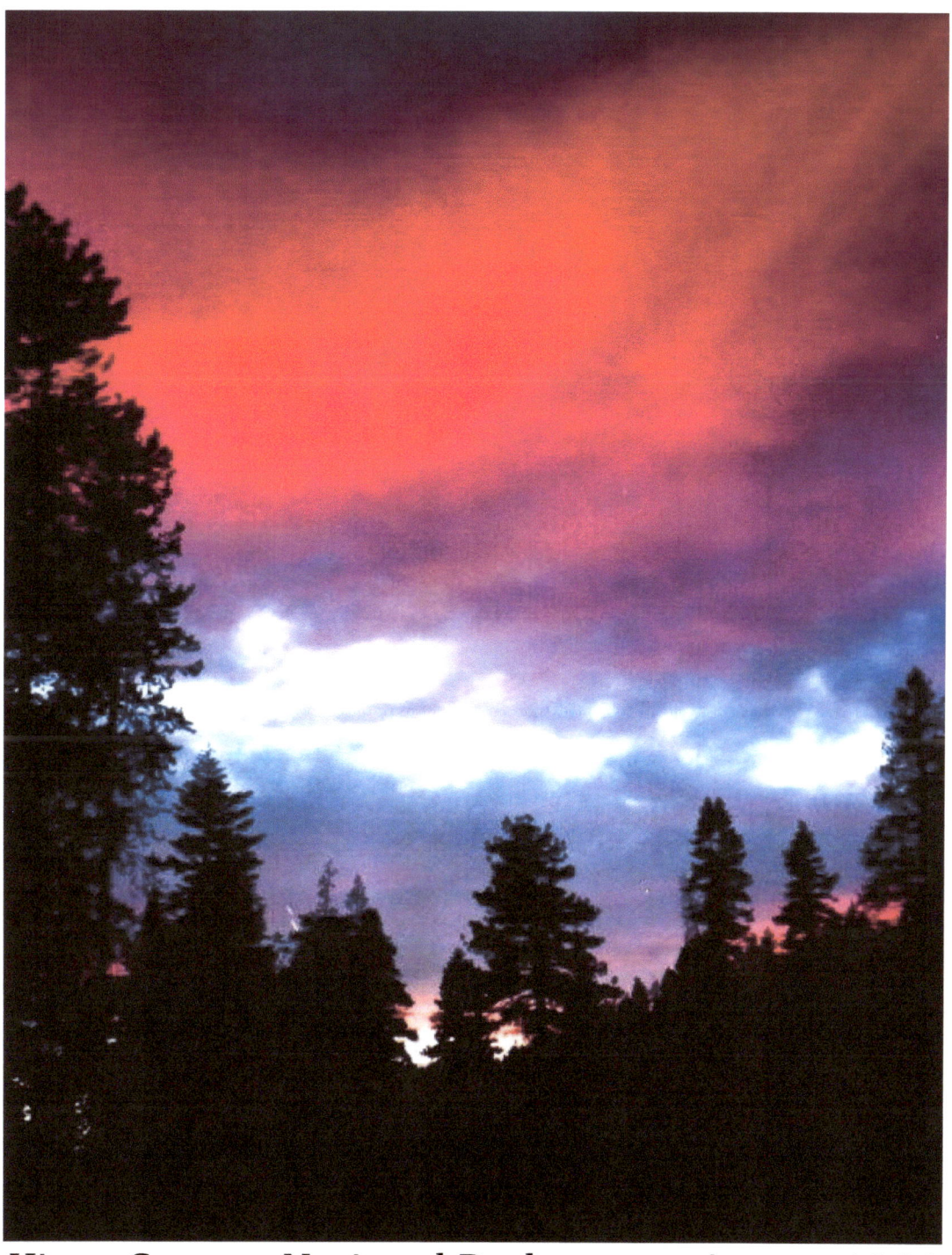

Kings Canyon National Park   August 1980

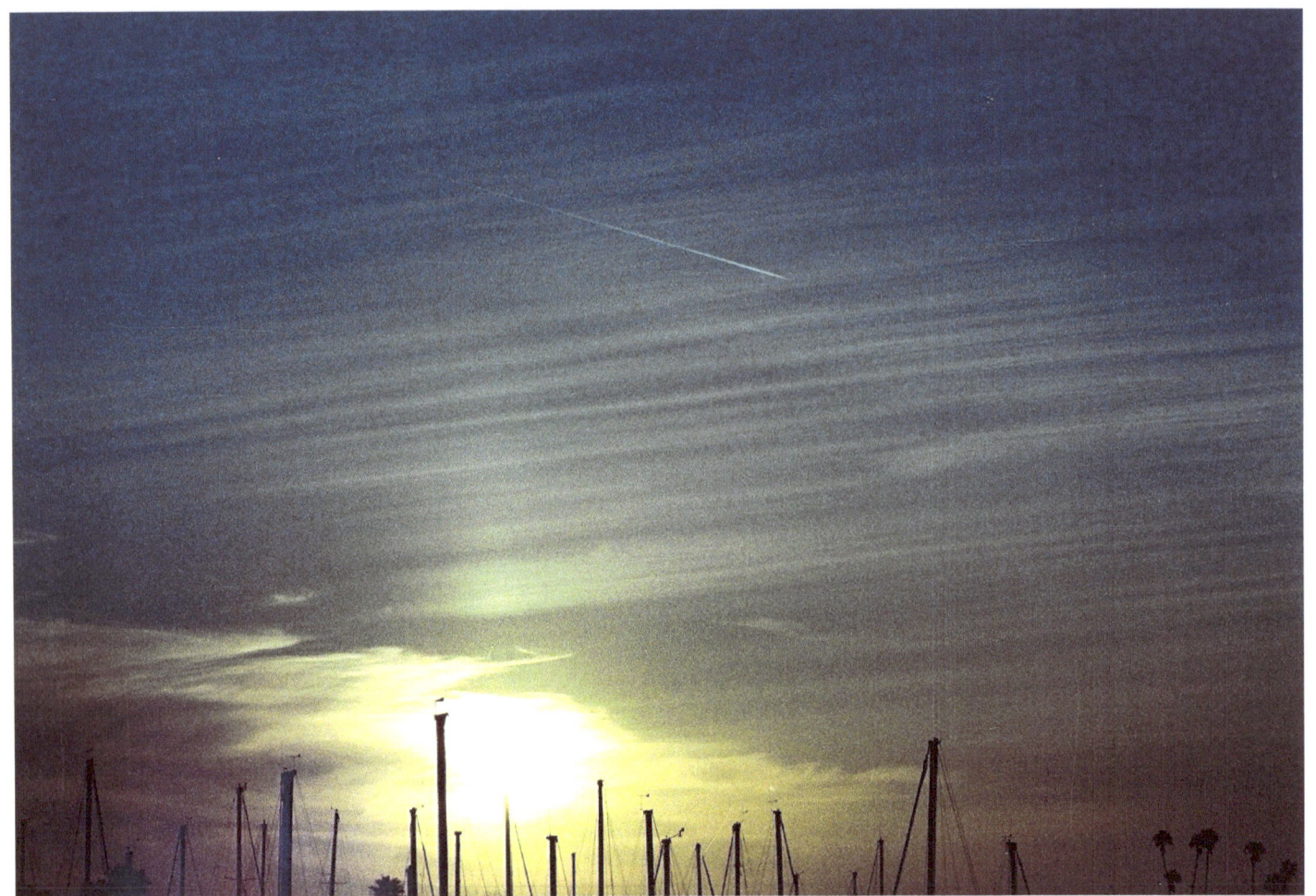

Oceanside Harbor, CA   May 1981

As I was shooting the masts of sailboats docked in the harbor of Oceanside, a meteor suddenly streaked through the evening sky. Without missing a beat, and knowing an opportunity like this would be hard pressed to come by, I quickly lifted my lens and took the shot.

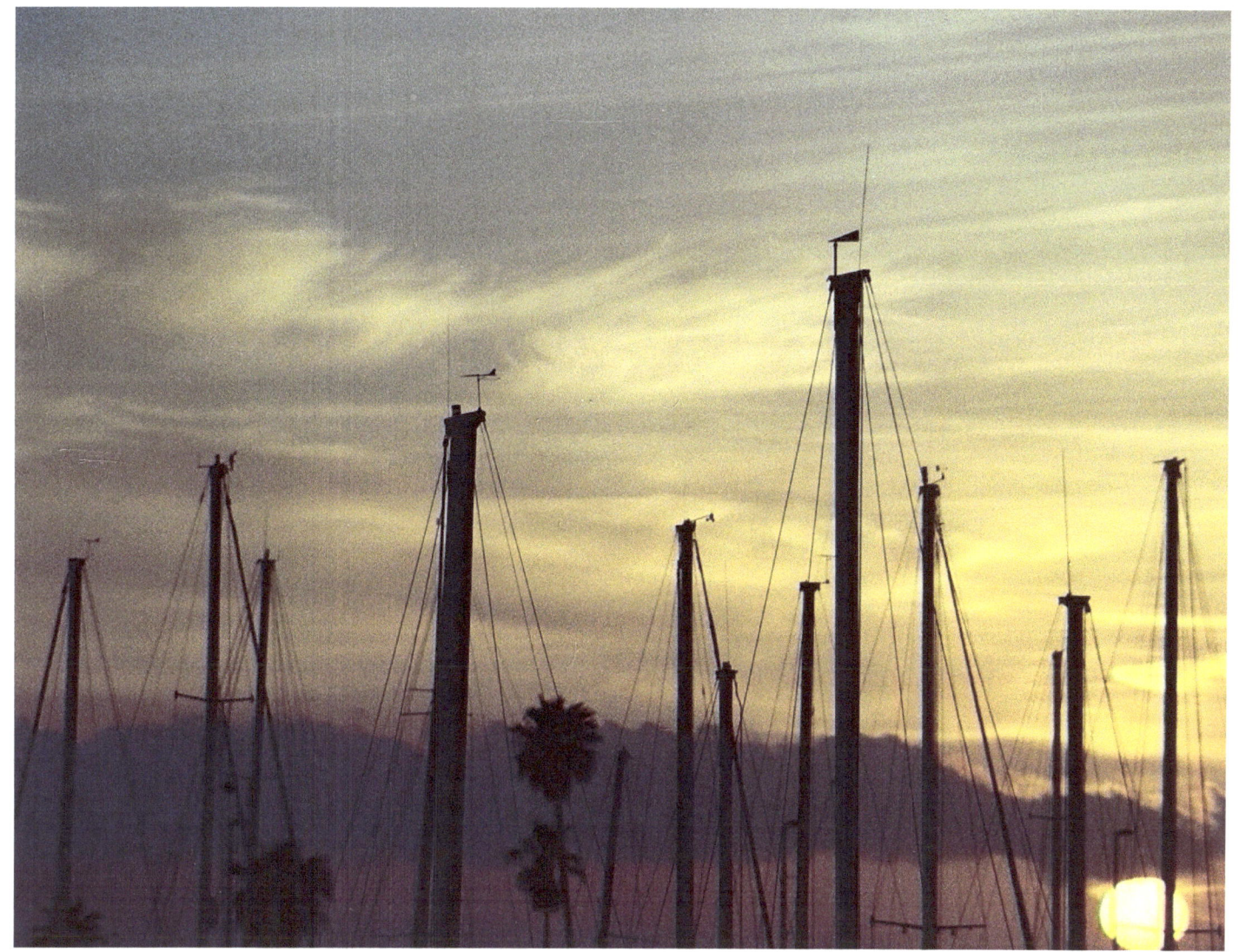

Oceanside Harbor, CA   May 1981

This was the shot I was after when the meteor passed by.

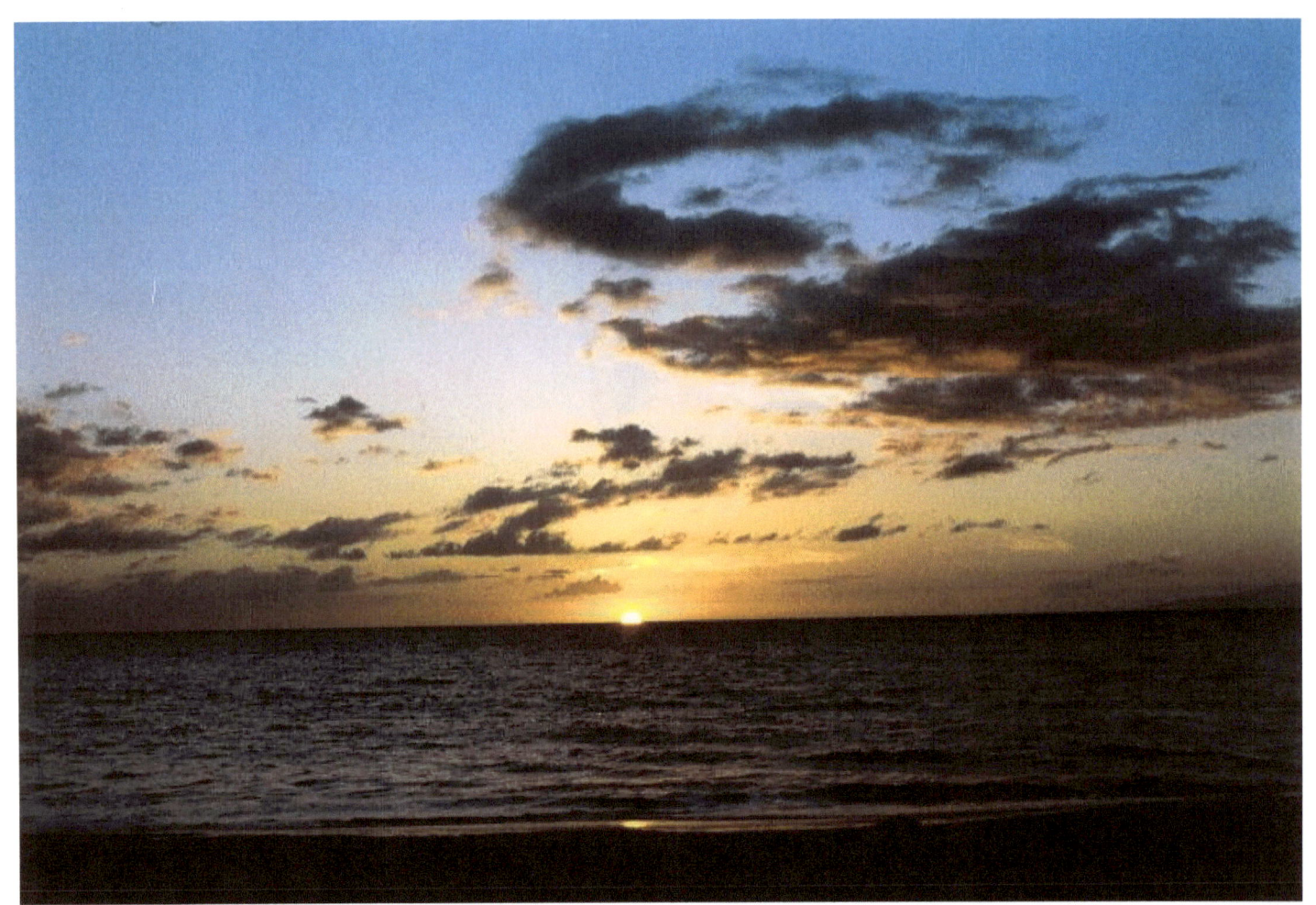

Maui, HI   December 2003

When working with sunsets and clouds, patience is of the essence. The colors
and lighting change almost instantaneously. Wait too long, you lose the shot,
too soon and it may not be the best shot. You can go through rolls of film this
way, but it can get expensive. Developing a good eye and patience will help you
get the best shot the first time.

This next shot was staged. I had an old baseball glove and the field was just a couple of blocks from me. It was late autumn and the shadows were getting longer. The season was over and win or lose, the pitcher had left his glove behind perhaps out of frustration, perhaps claiming the mound as his after a winning season.

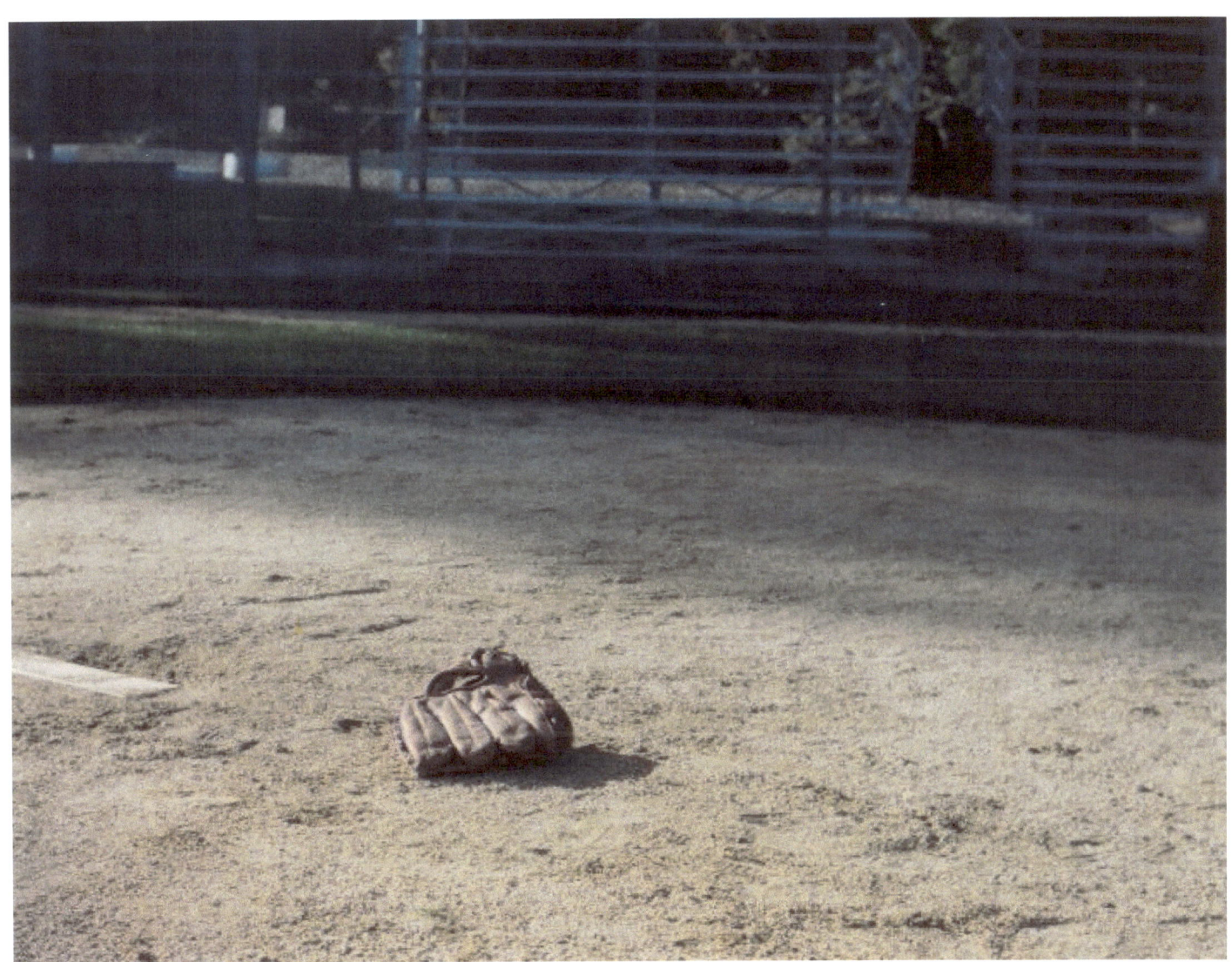

Camera

Ready

Being camera ready means always having your camera with you. If you are working in 35mm, that means one camera with color film and another with black and white.

I have a bumper sticker that reads; "this car stops for photo-ops," for if I see a shot, or the potential for one, I have been known to swing the car to the right and stop, fly out with camera in hand and take it, or get ready for it. Be safe as you are driving but remember there might be a great photo-op around the next corner.

Even when walking down the street, throw your camera bag over your shoulder like a woman carries her purse. You may think it's cumbersome, but not having it is when the great photo-op presents itself can be agonizing. If you are a woman, make some room in your purse, or develop a bag where camera and your essentials can live side by side.

Don't have a camera bag? Get one, as you will find that having your camera extras with you can provide you with the shot you're looking for. This may include; lenses, filters, cleaning supplies and, of course, extra film for your 35 mm. I know many digital photographers that still carry a 35 mm camera around.

At any rate, if you're serious about photography, then be prepared.

The following are some photo-ops I was lucky enough to encounter.

Solo Flight, Leucadia, CA 2009

Standing on the bluffs of Leucadia, CA overlooking the beach and ocean, I noticed this pelican cruising the thermals heading straight for me.

Poised with camera, I followed it until it had made its way past me and just past the setting sun.

This was a once click shot. The chances of another one coming along anytime soon were slim to none.

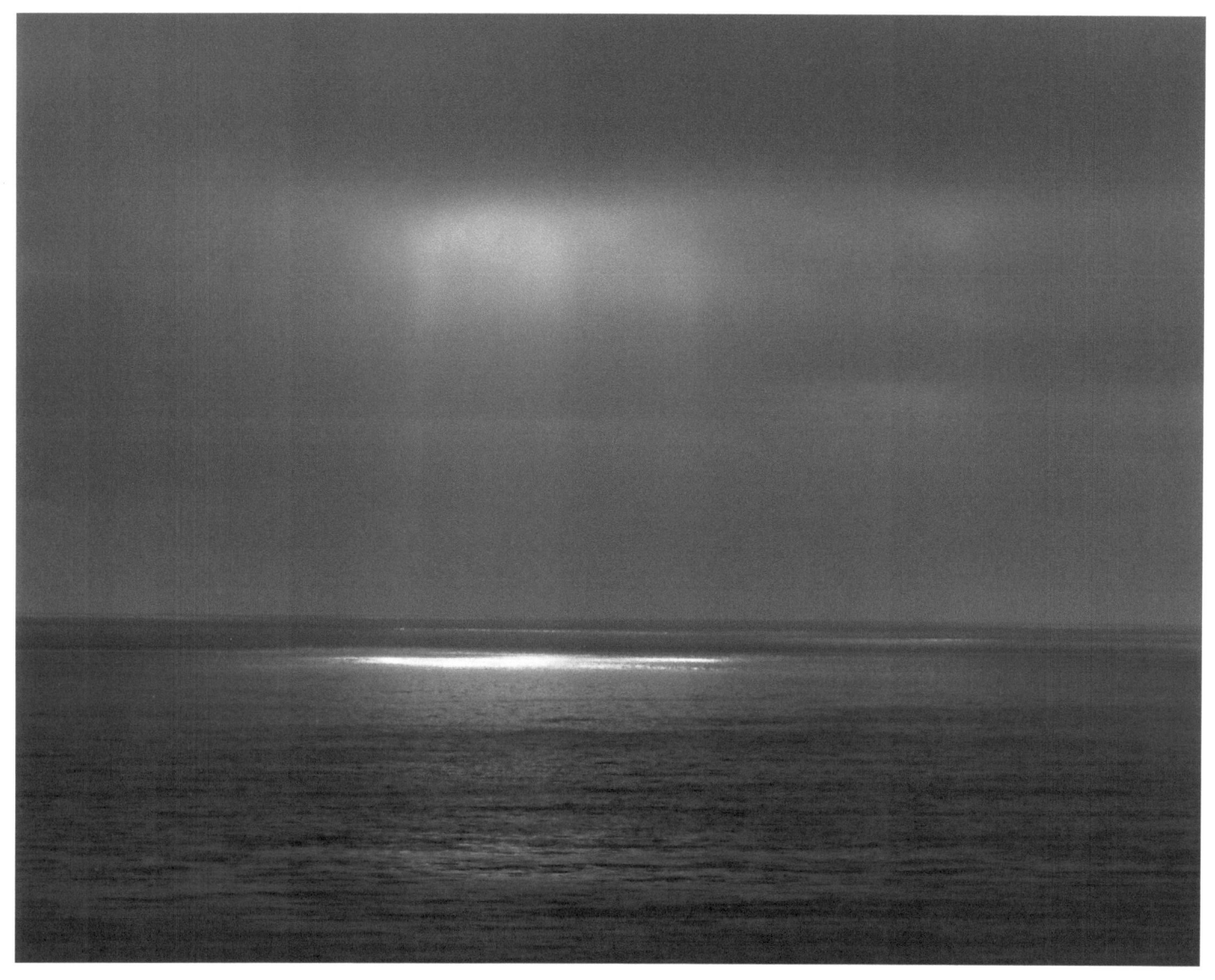

"Let There Be Light" – Carlsbad, CA 2009

On cloudy days, the sun may find a way to peek through and shed its light, this time on the waters of the Pacific, making a spectacular scene; and as one might imagine, courtesy of a higher power.

These moments don't last forever or can be quite as dramatic, hence, being camera ready can produce some wonderful shots.

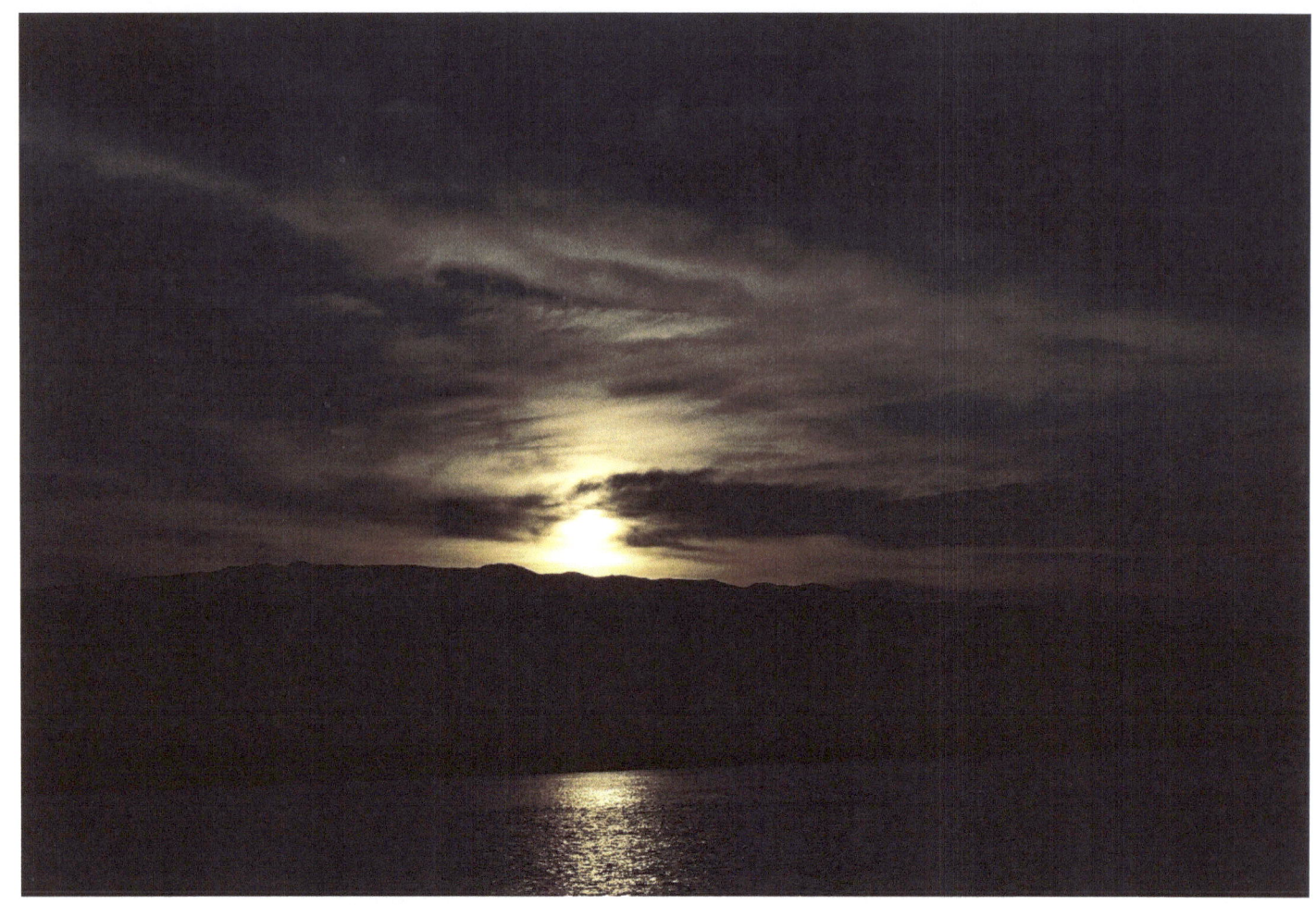

Silhouette Sunset – Maui, 2001

I was having a late lunch, or possibly an early supper, at Cheeseburger in Paradise in Lahina, Maui, when outside my window this spectacular sunset began its show; silhouetting the island of Lanai while casting its glow on the waters between us. The clouds only added to the design of the night.

When you go out to eat and want a window seat, there must be a reason, and usually it's the view. Don't be one of those who wish they had brought a camera with them.

Yes, it's true that camera phones are improving all the time, but still can't compete with professional grade equipment at this time.

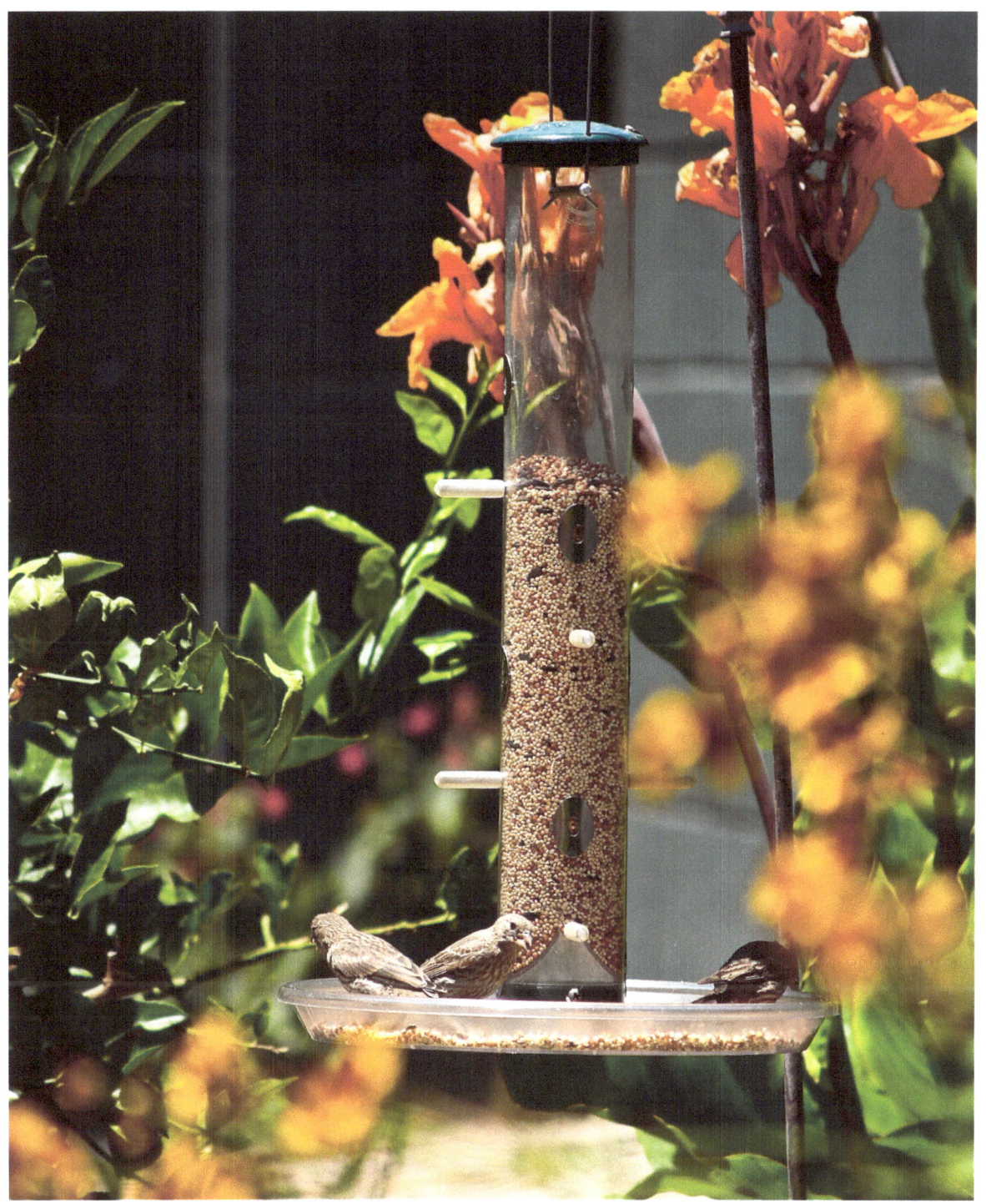

Dinner is Served – Queen Creek, AZ 2010

Birds and other wild creatures certainly are not going to wait for you to go into the house to find a camera. If you've taken the time to set up a staging area to attract wild life, then take the time to have your camera ready too.

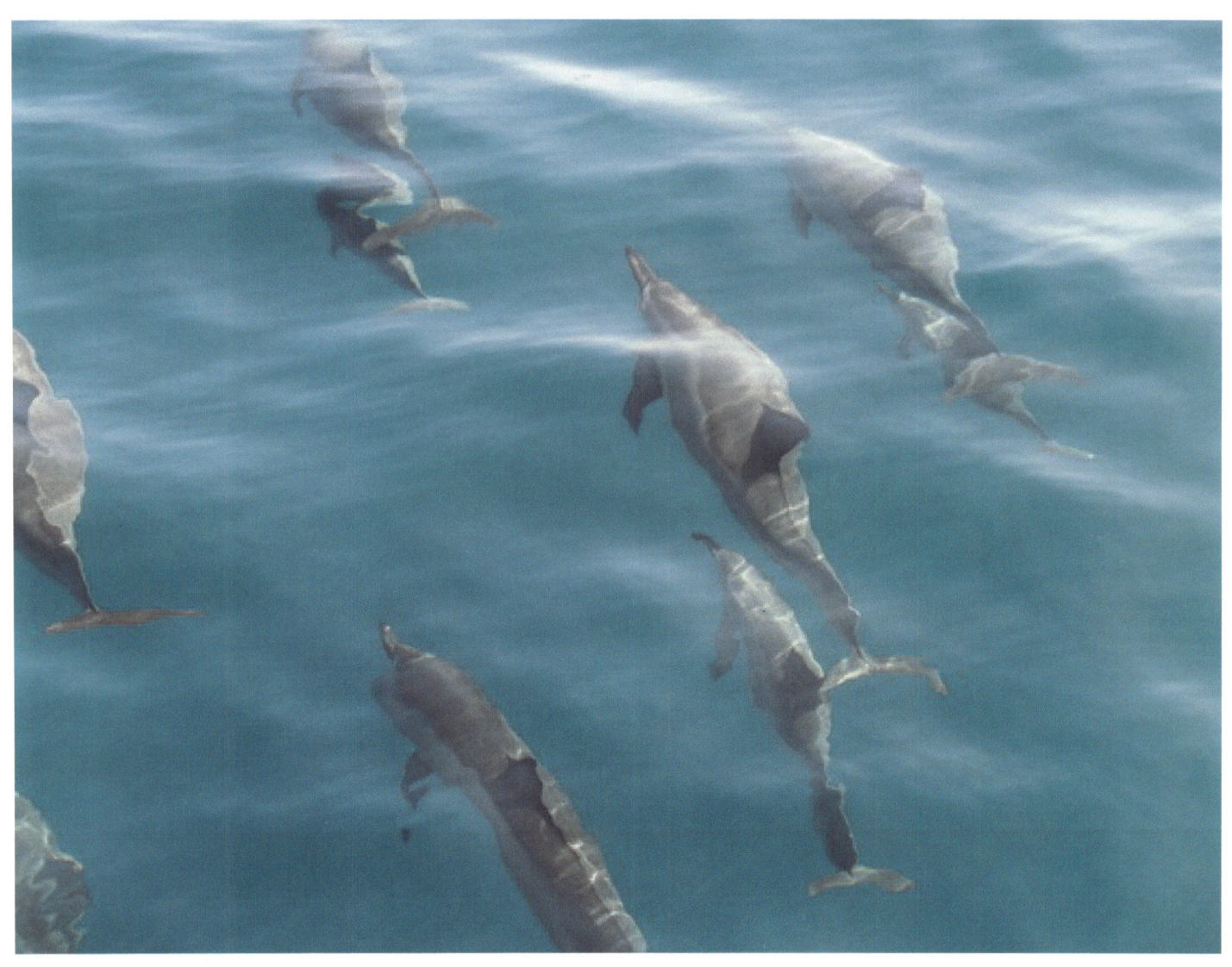

Spinner Dolphins – Kauai, 2006

Once again a unique opportunity presented itself while touring off the island of Kauai. The water so clear making this shot possible. And, of course, I was camera ready.

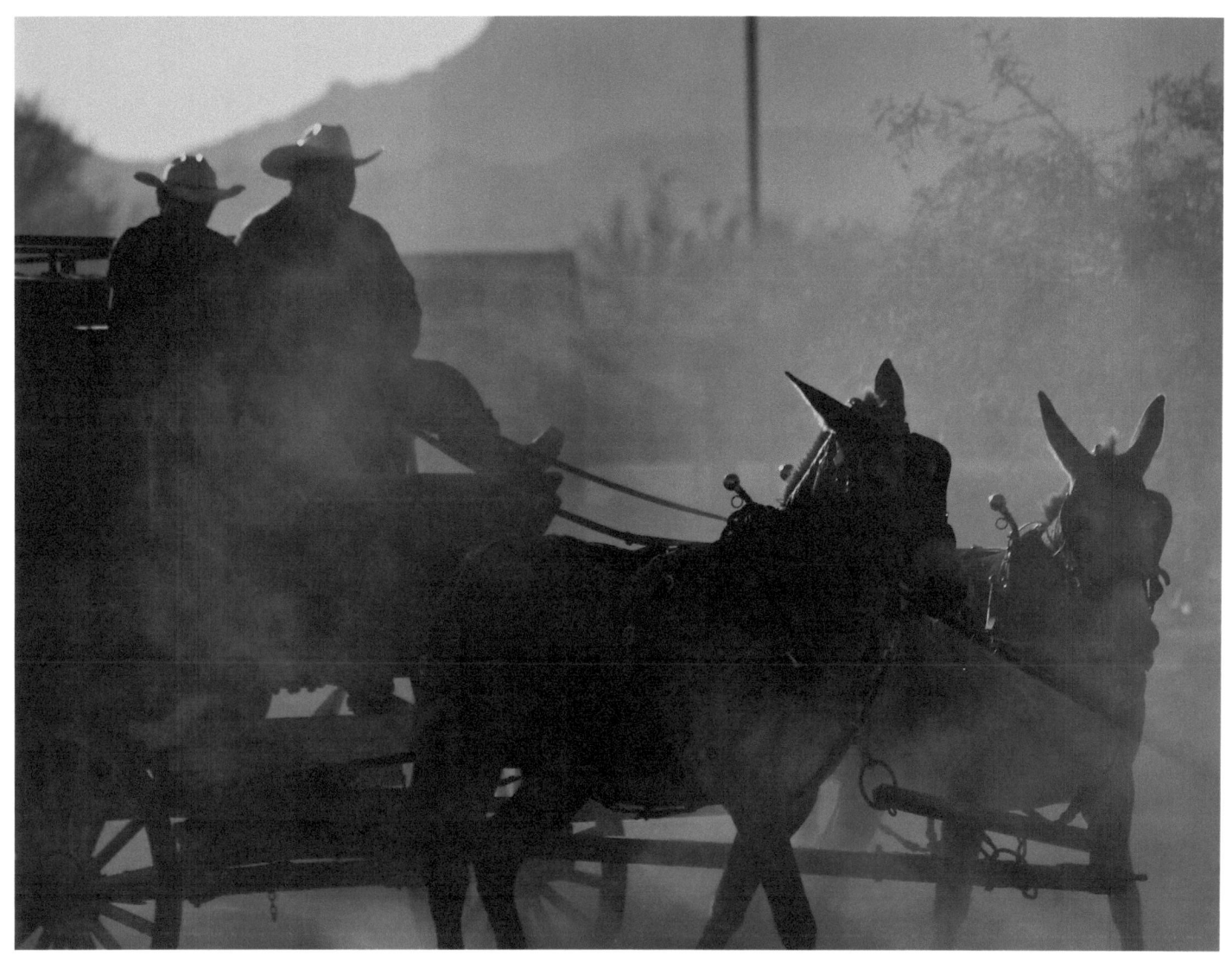

Comin' In – Rawhide, AZ 2011

By land, air or sea, your eyes must always be open to the potential great shot before it's gone. You just never know what's up around the next bend. So keep your eyes on the horizon and your finger on the trigger.

Oddities

Shooting something different for kicks and giggles or just to practice a skill.

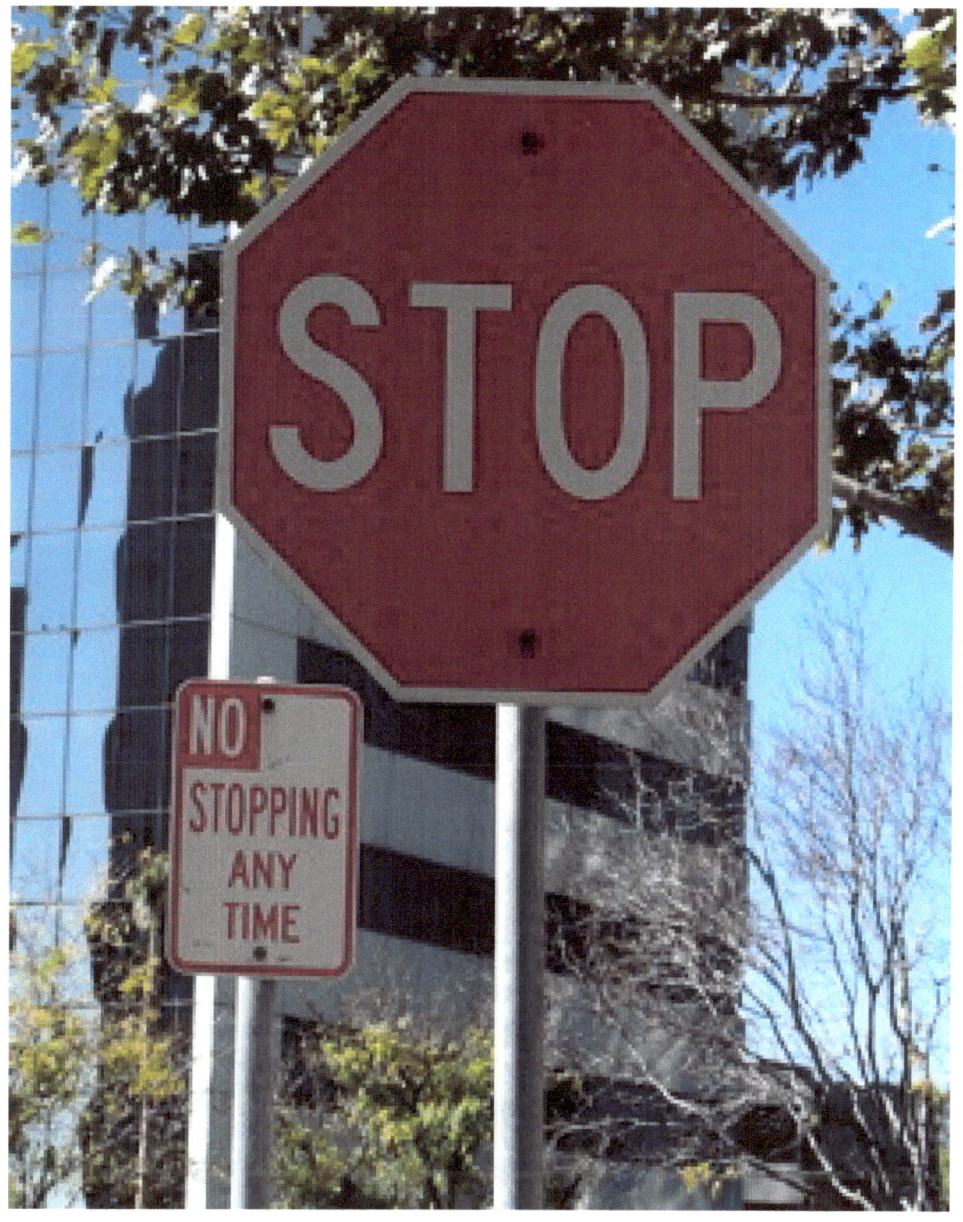

Sometimes there are those things in life that need to be recorded for posterity.
This is the epitome of a beauracratic society.

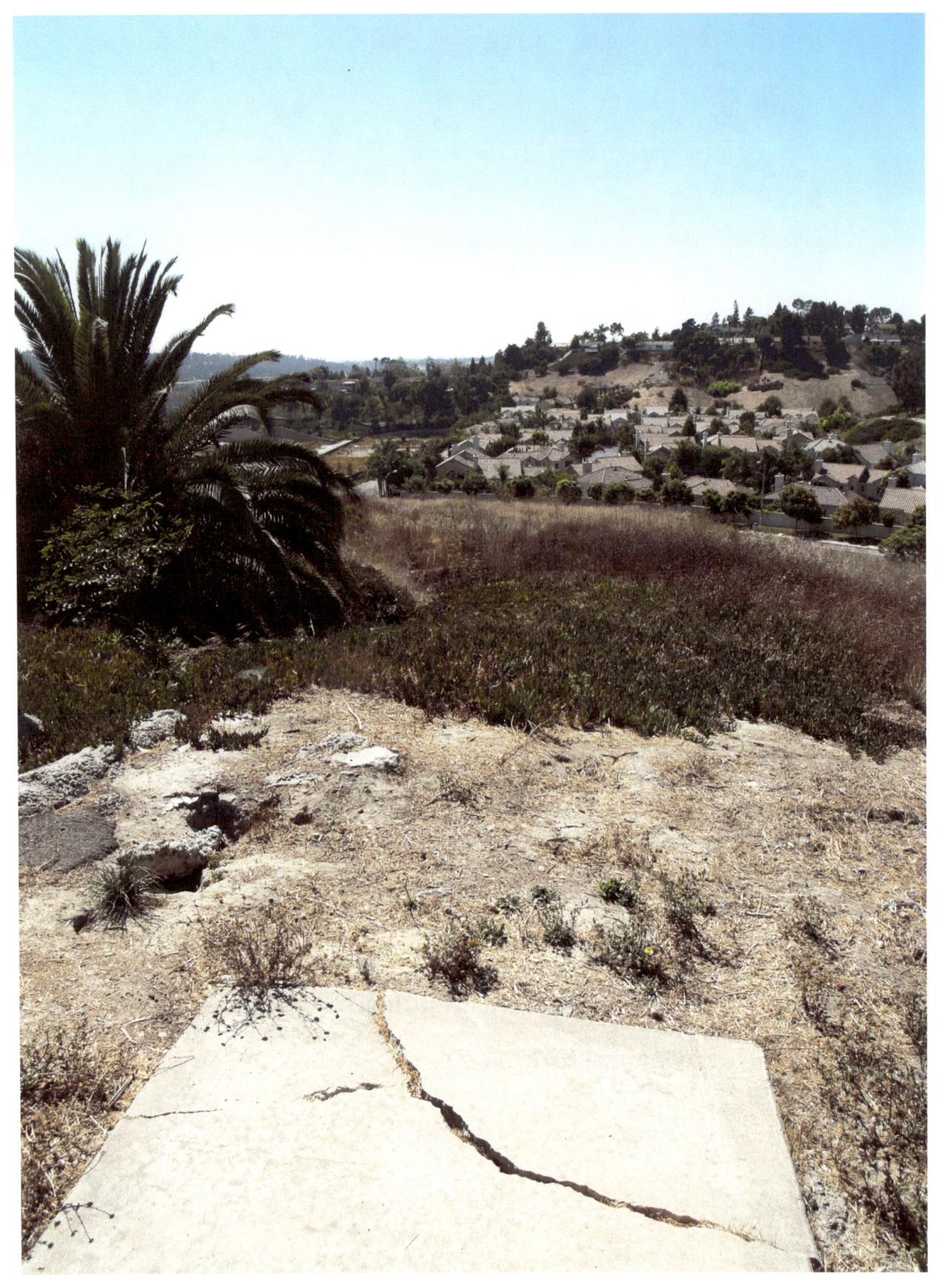

Where the sidewalk ends. A tribute to Shel Silverstein.

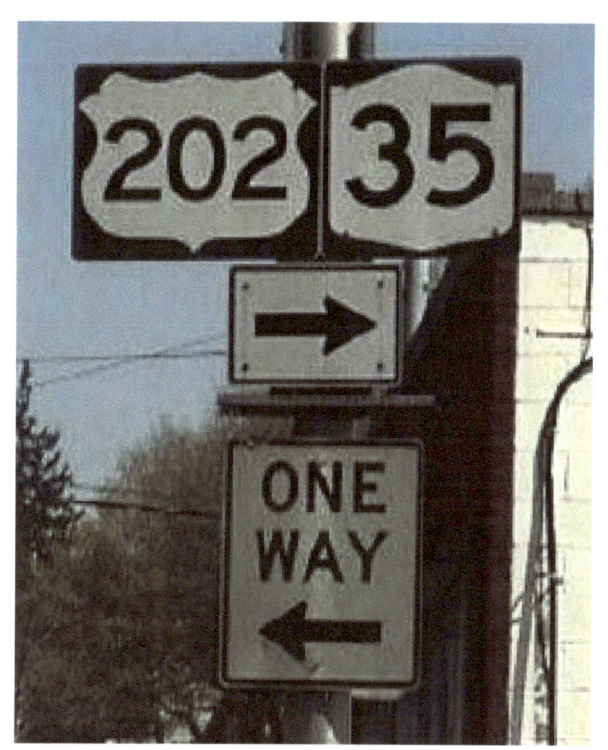

But, how do I...?

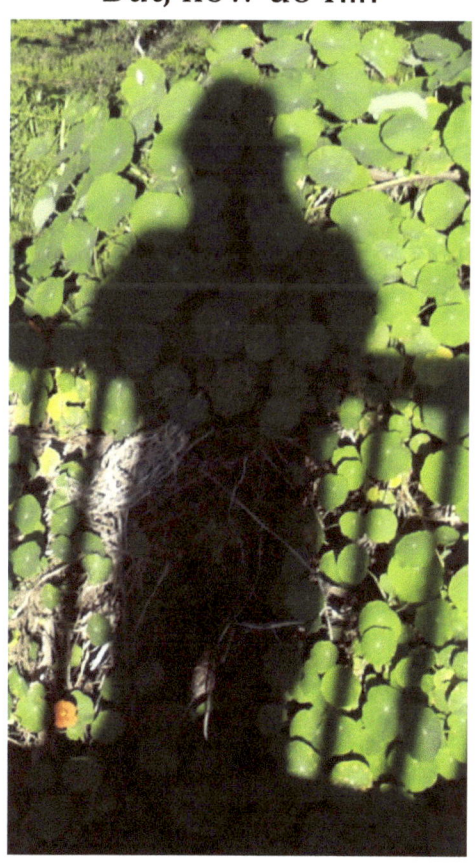

Shadow of a Man

The

People

Factor

Why shooting as second banana has its benefits.

   If someone were to ask me if I'd like the lead photography position at an important event, such as a wedding, I would pass in a heart beat. The reason? Too much pressure to get everyone together in a timely and organized way and take the perfect shots for wedding albums and keepsakes.

The following pics were done as second photographer, catching those keepsake moments as random and spontaneous.

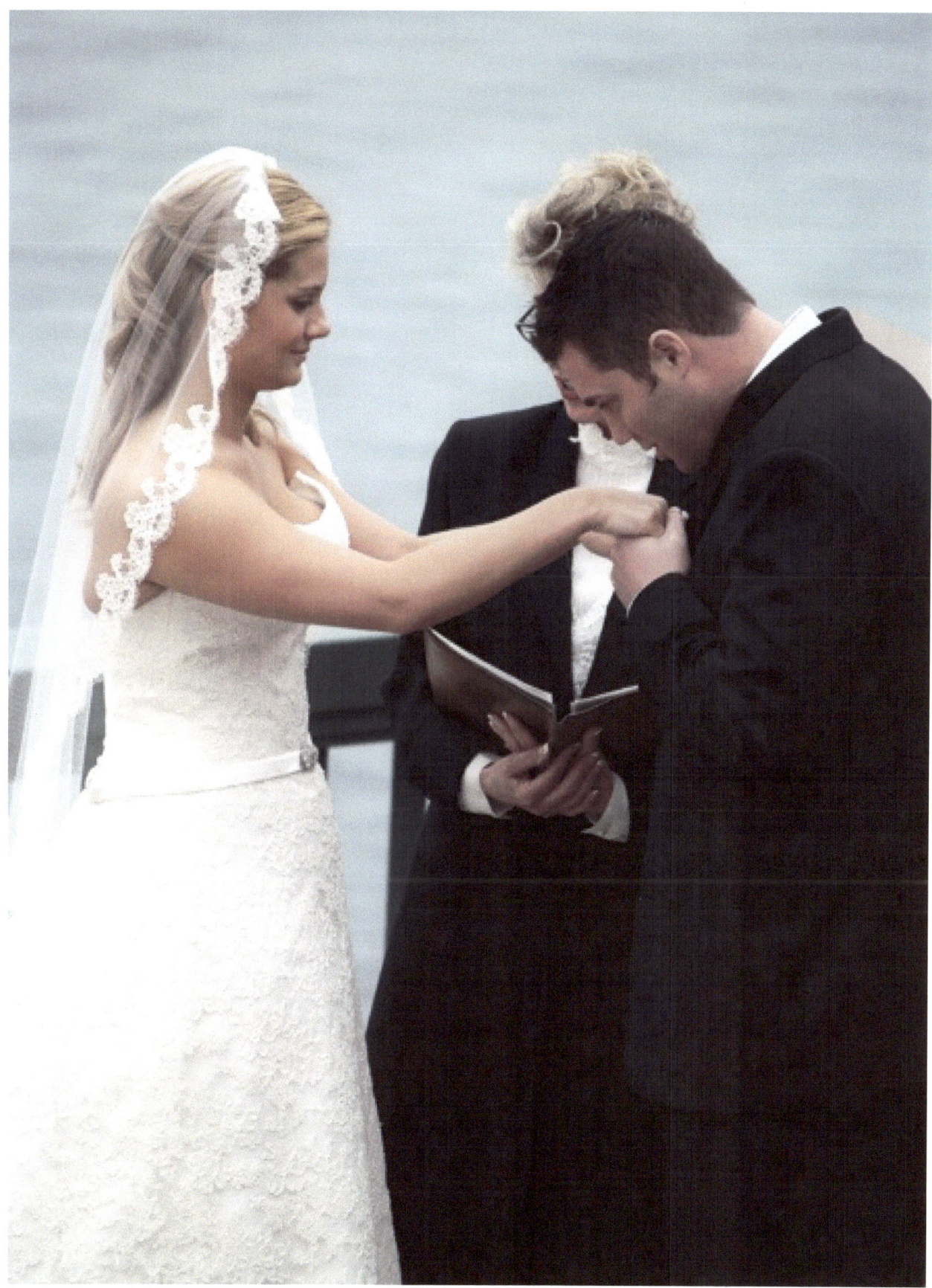

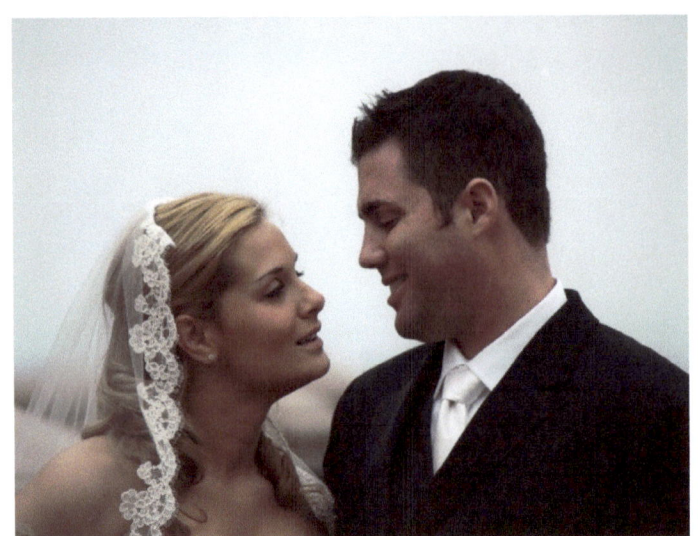

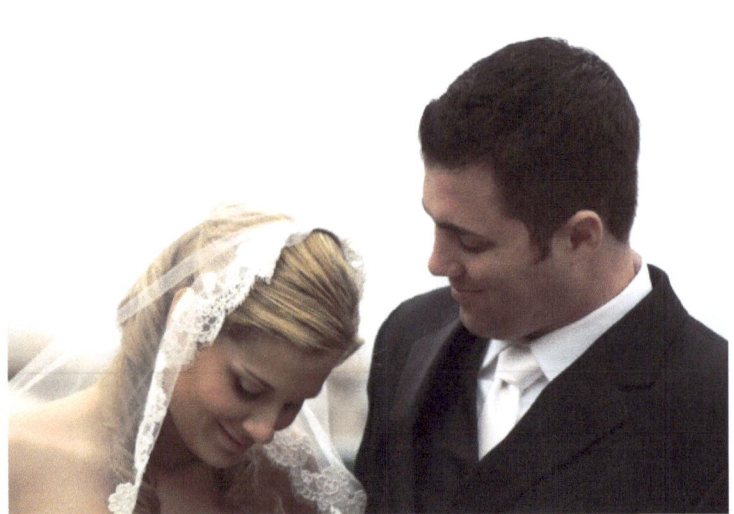

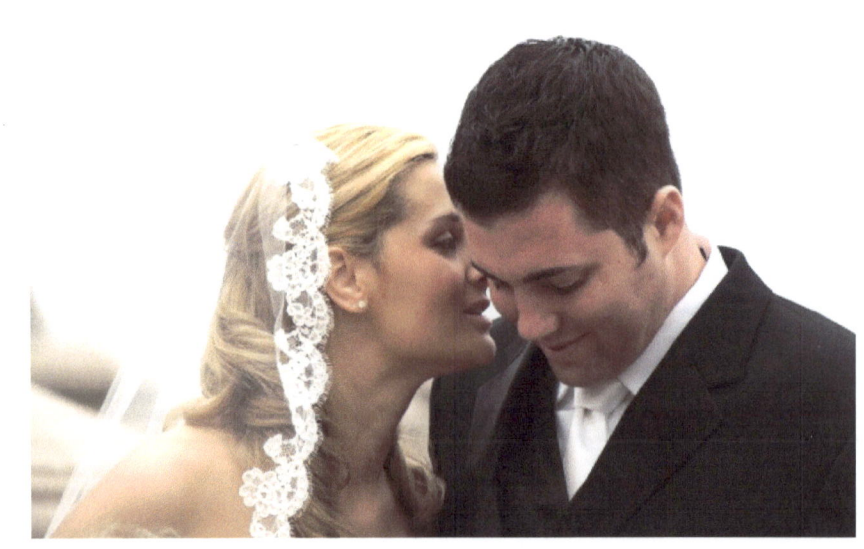

Sometimes a shot needs to be created.

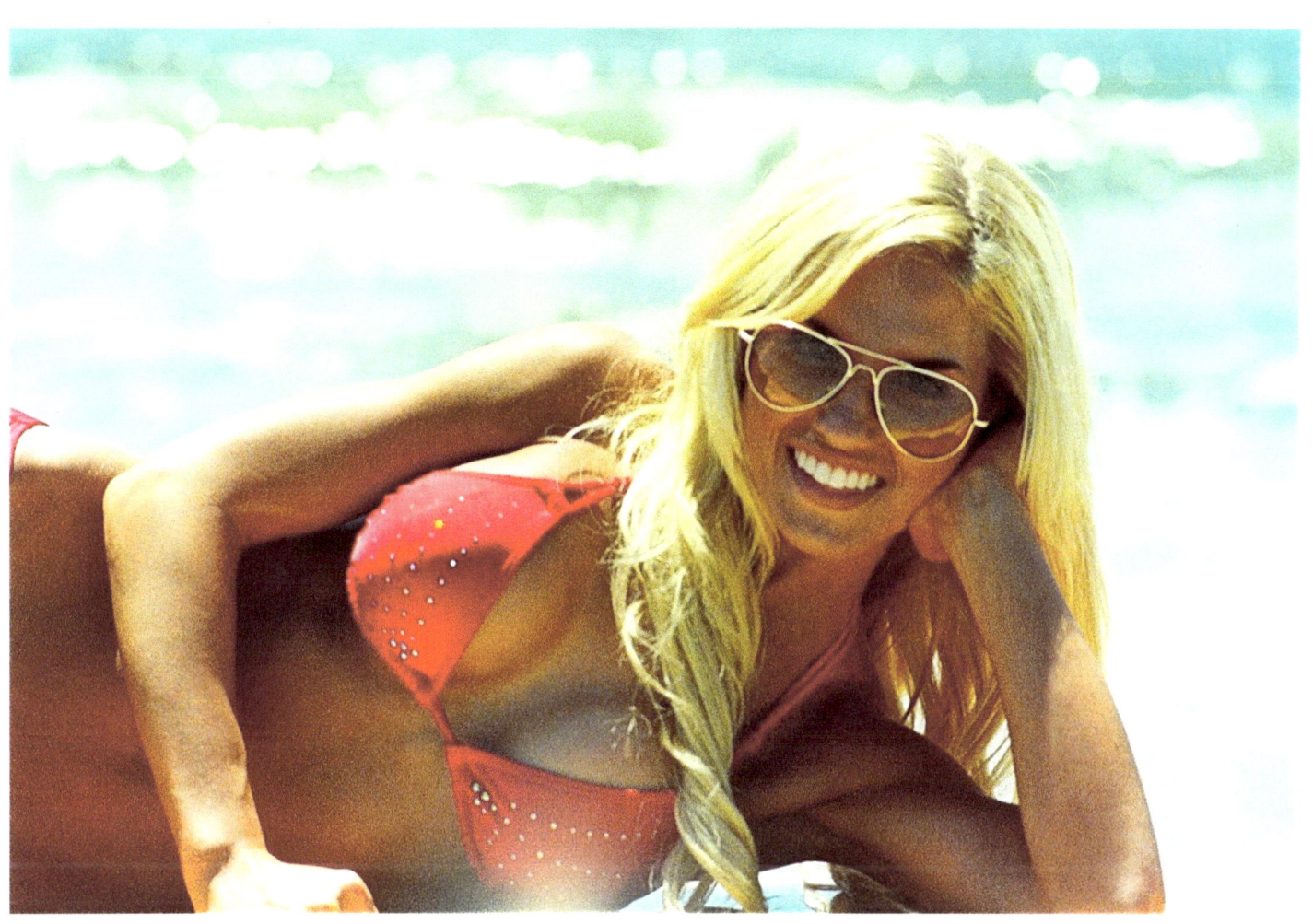

Golden Girl – Santa Cruz, CA, 2008

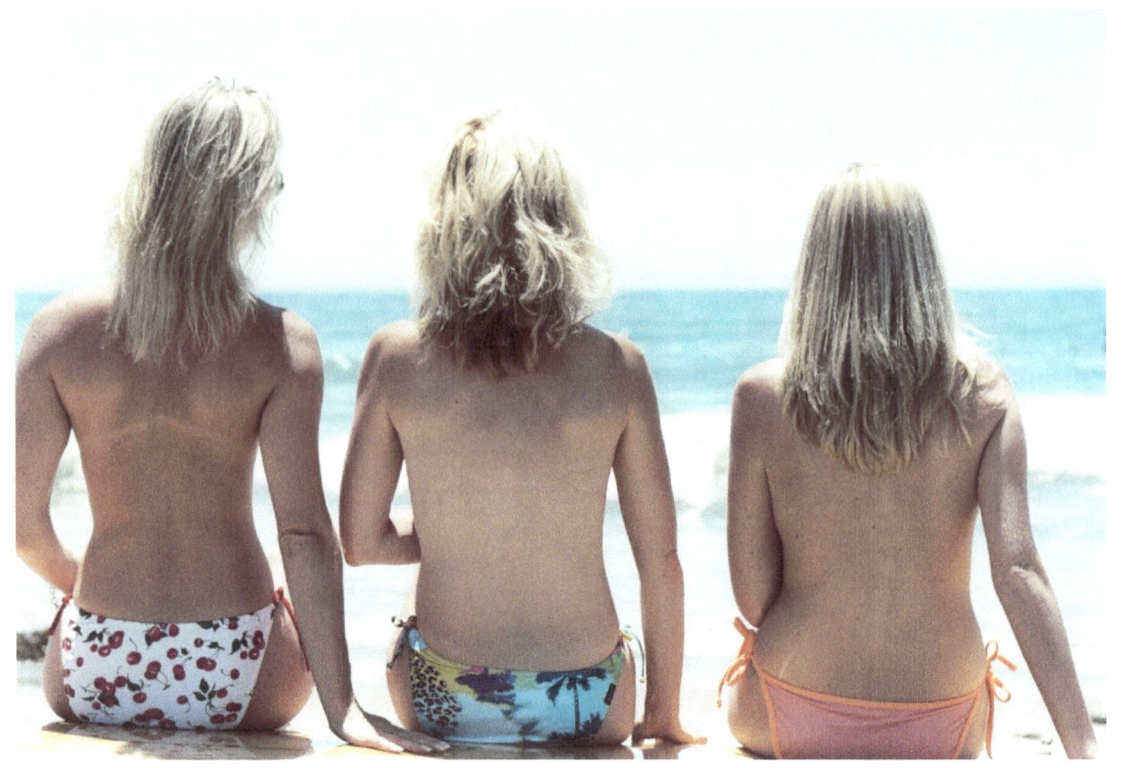

Beached Blondes – Santa Cruz, 2008

The beach gals were done as a photo shoot for Tommy Tahiti. Though I prefer to do my own shoots and sell them as fine art, sometimes an interesting project comes along that also pays the rent. I'm not so prideful as to turn down commercial work.

Getting

Lucky

But it's not only patience and good subject matter that results in quality photos, but sometimes it's what's happening in the now and accidentally running across it, as in the following photos.

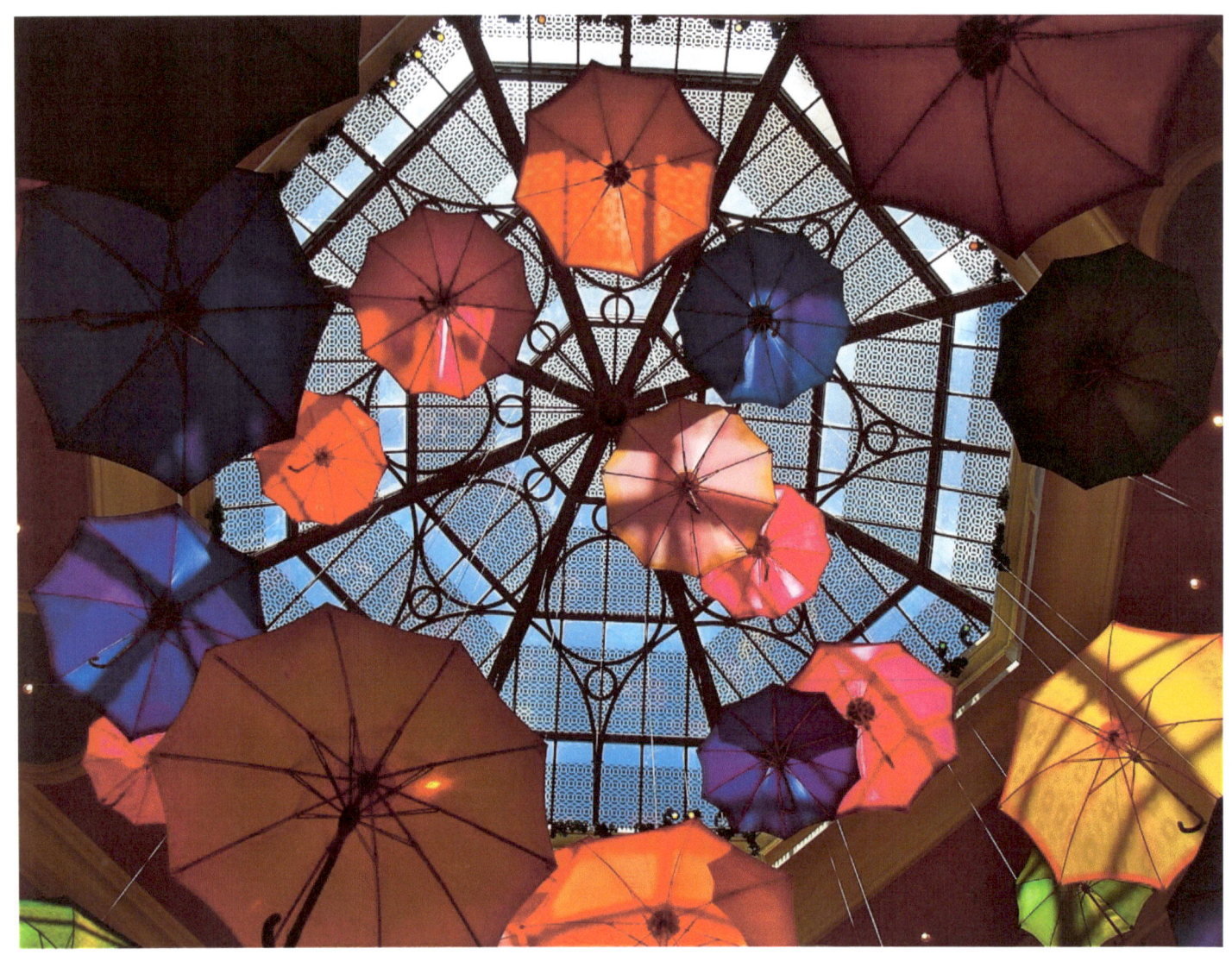

Salute to Poppins – Bellagio, Las Vegas 2010

A spontaneous trip to Vegas yielded this photo, as hundreds of umbrellas were open and hung throughout the hotel and shopping areas.

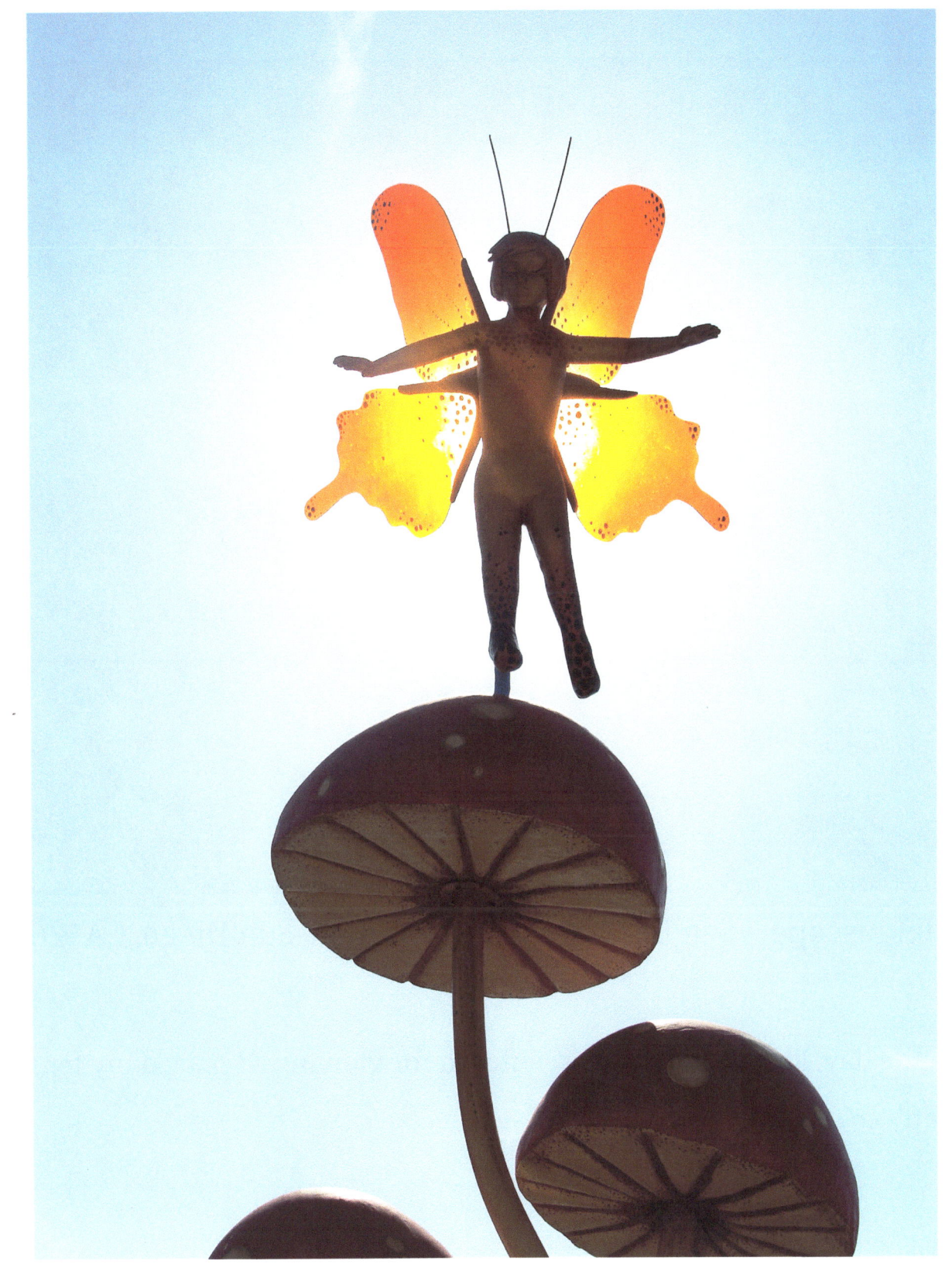

Sun Fairy – San Diego Beach boardwalk, San Diego, CA 2008

A walk down the San Diego Beach boardwalk saw other types of art projects. I positioned my camera so the sun would illuminate the fairy.

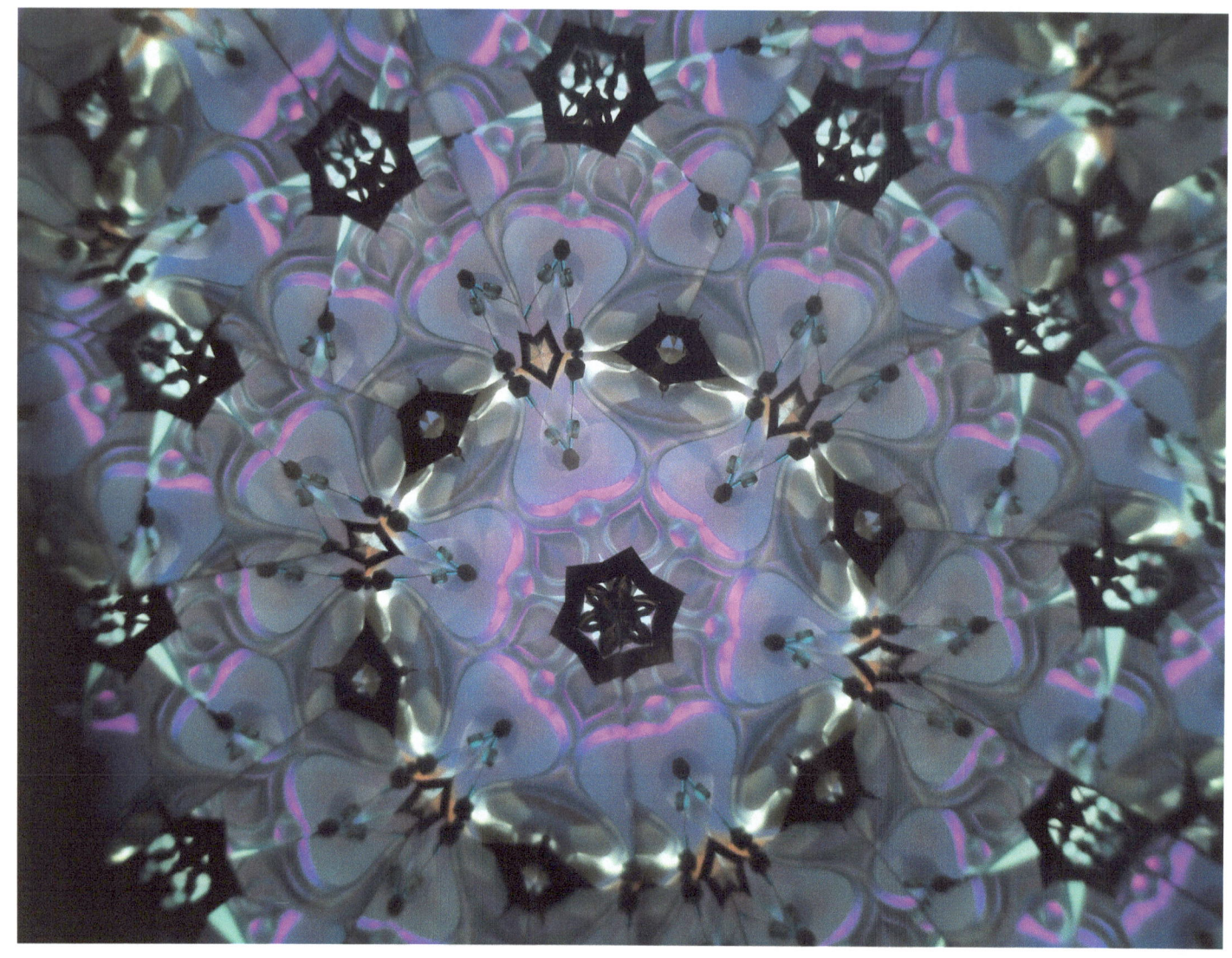

Kaleidoscope – San Diego Beach Boardwalk, San Diego, CA 2008

That same day, kaleidoscopes were offered for viewing.   I placed my lens over the eyepiece and took this shot.

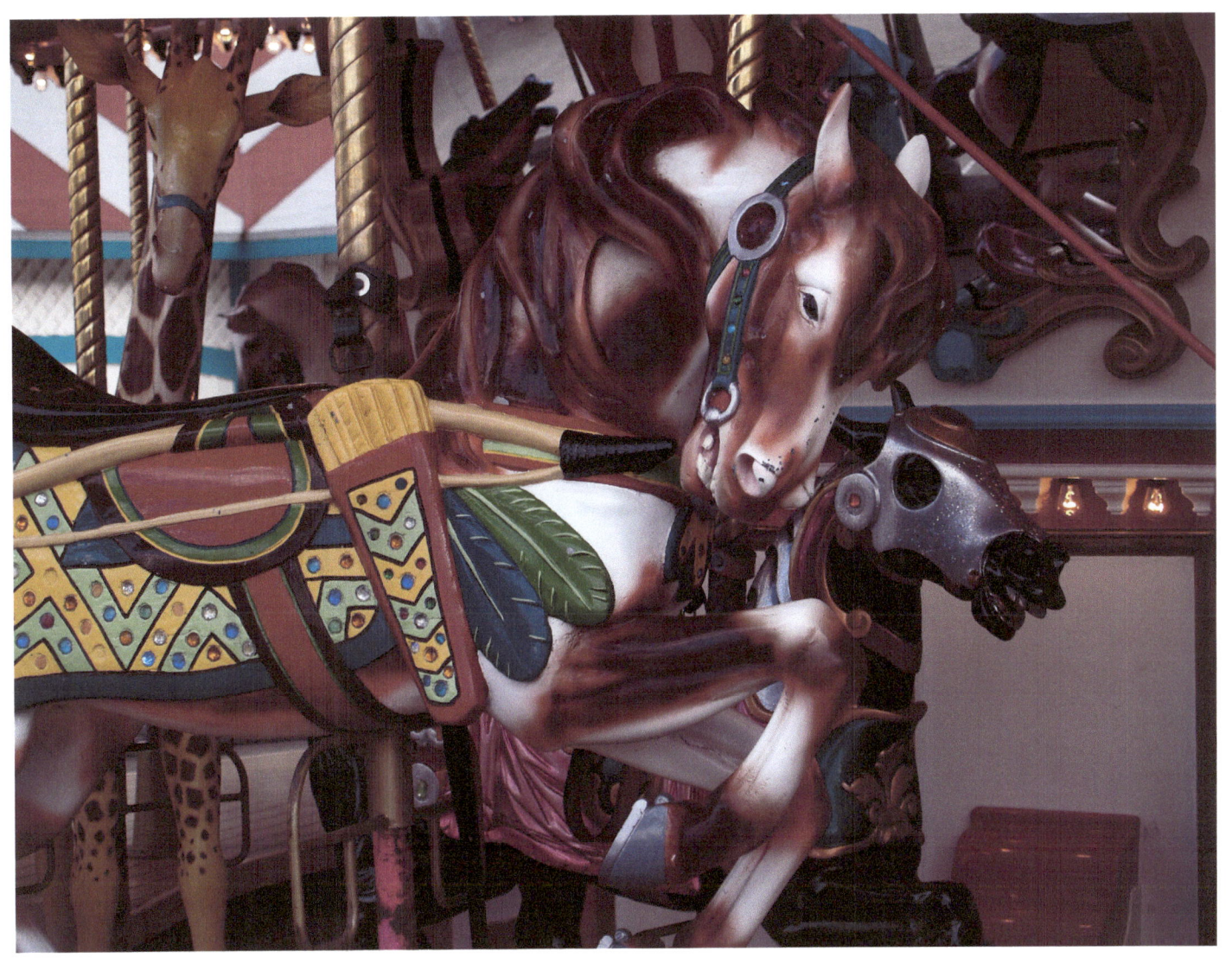

Painted Ponies – Mission Beach, San Diego, CA 2008

San Diego's Mission Beach district offers an old fashion theme park with a carousel, roller coaster and more. The opportunity for photographs is almost endless.

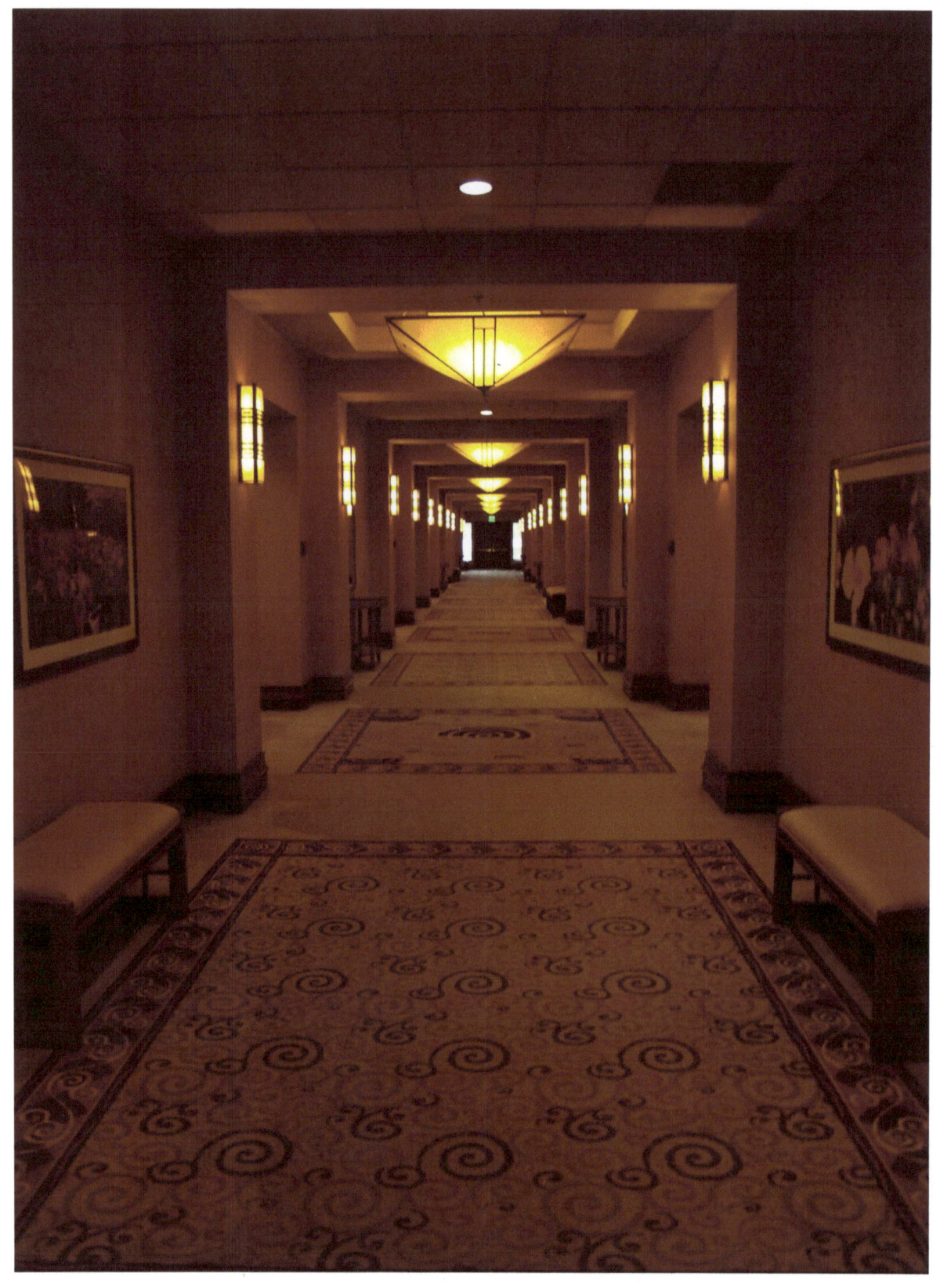

The Hall – Pacheco, CA, 2009

Sometimes places where you stay offer a unique perspective if you look closely. This hallway caught my eye as to the repetitiveness of it as well the length allowing it to do so.

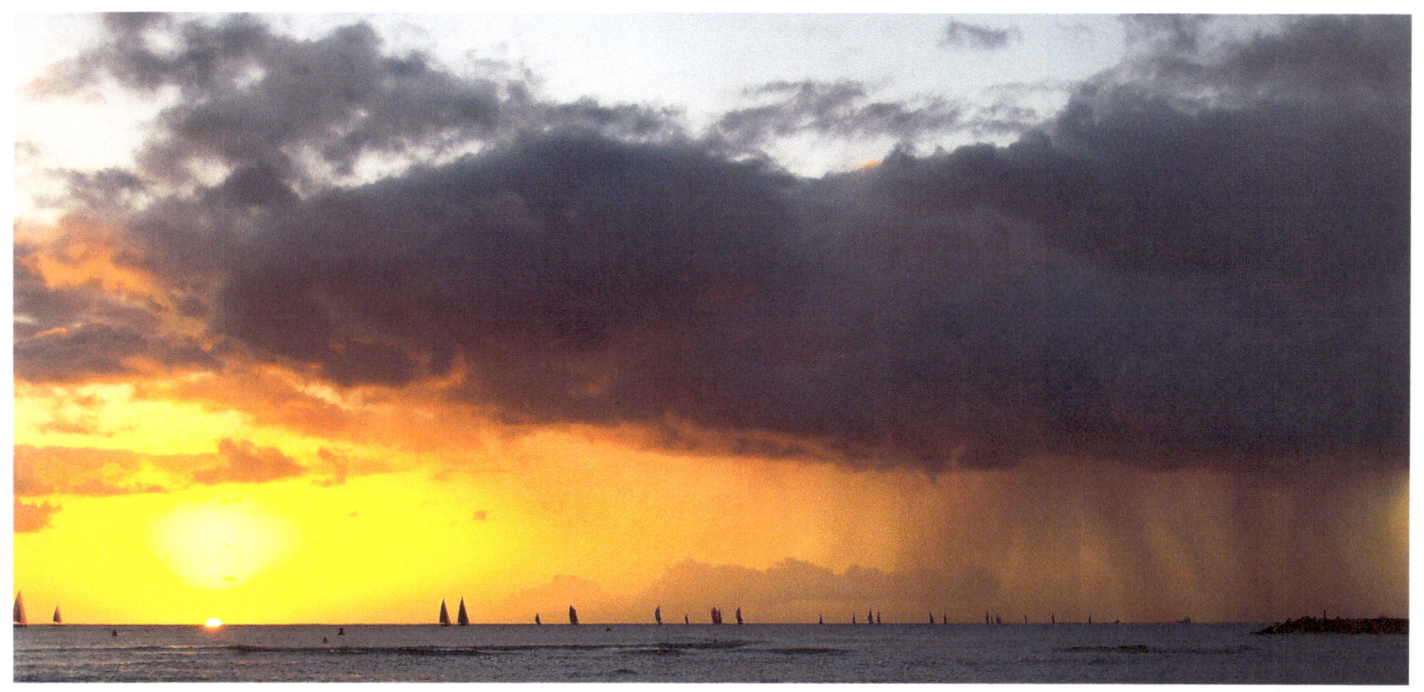

Weather or Not – Oahu, Hawaii 2007

Off the coast of Honolulu was a small regatta of sailboats just far enough away where, using my panorama lens, I was able to capture a late afternoon storm and the sunset.

Sometimes a photographer is just blessed to be in the right time and place.

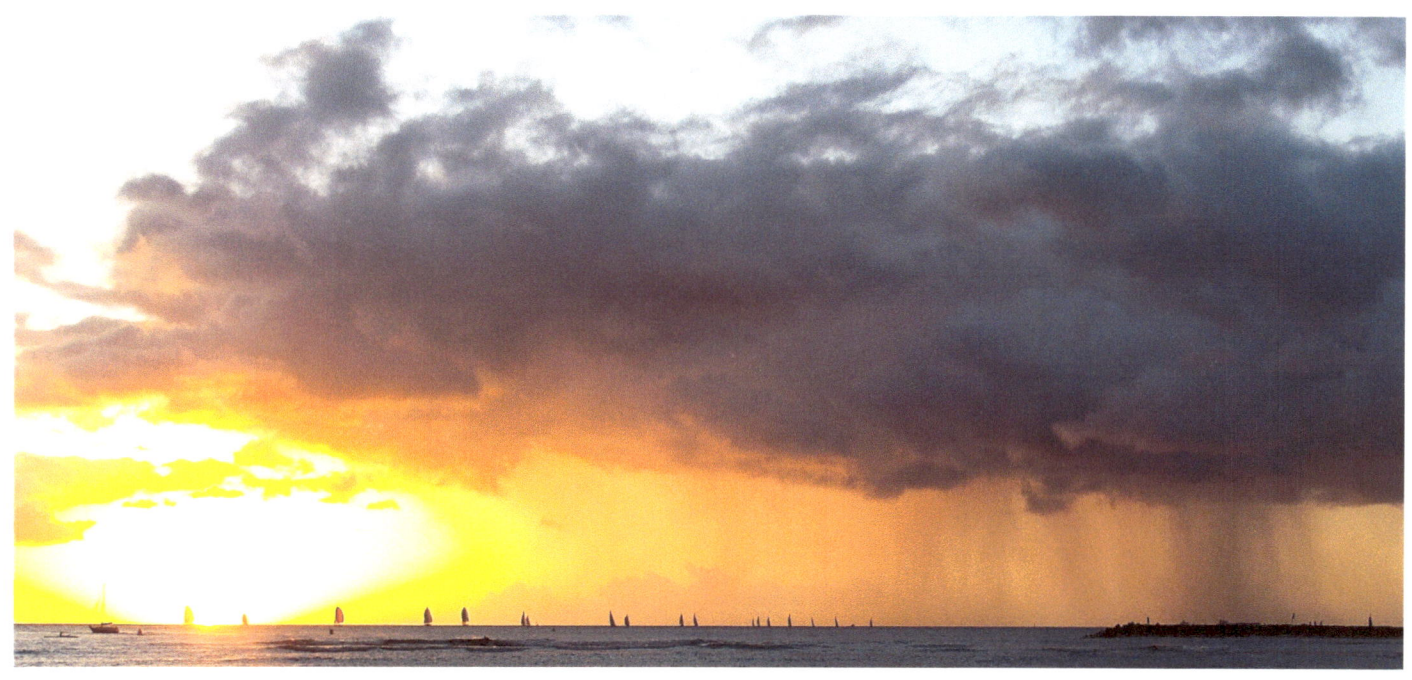

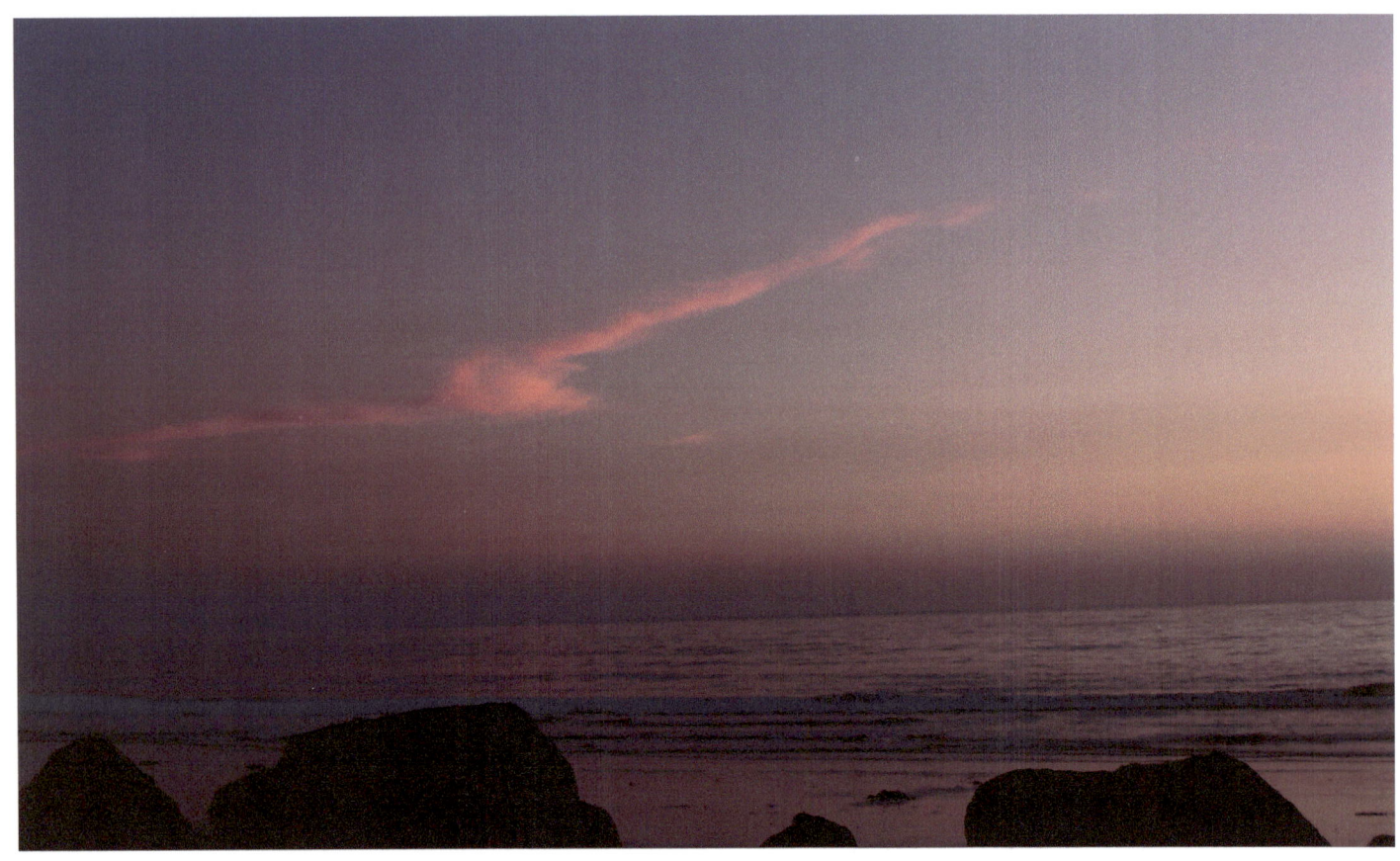

Cloud Bird – Cardiff-by-the-Sea, 2008

If we are observant (and as photographers we should be) we find Mother Nature works with us giving the opportunity for some beautiful and unique shots.

While waiting for dinner reservations, I spotted this cloud shaped like a bird taking flight out to sea. I shot its farewell journey, more than likely never to be seen again.

Nudes: A Somewhat Difficult Subject

In the summers of 1999 and 2000 I decided to try my photographic skills in shooting nudes. Still using a 35 mm camera, this proved to be the ultimate test of patience since other humans were involved in the success of these photos while in the others, my own patience was tested.

As an aside, all models were 18 or older at the time of the shoot, were paid and signed a release form that I still have on file today. Models got to choose whether they wanted to remain anonymous or not. Since the focus, in black and white, was to view the shape of a woman, her curves and lines, shooting a model from the neck down was not a problem. I made sure that all photos were in good taste as there are a few critics out there who can't distinguish art from pornography. I certainly hope you can.

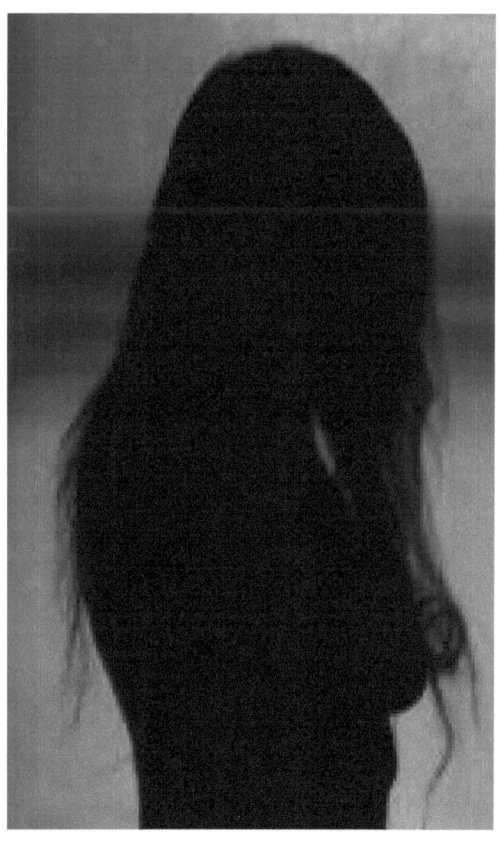

Silhouette of a Woman 2009

The backside of a woman can be just as intriguing as any other part. Notice the curves and lines that make her a "thing" of beauty.

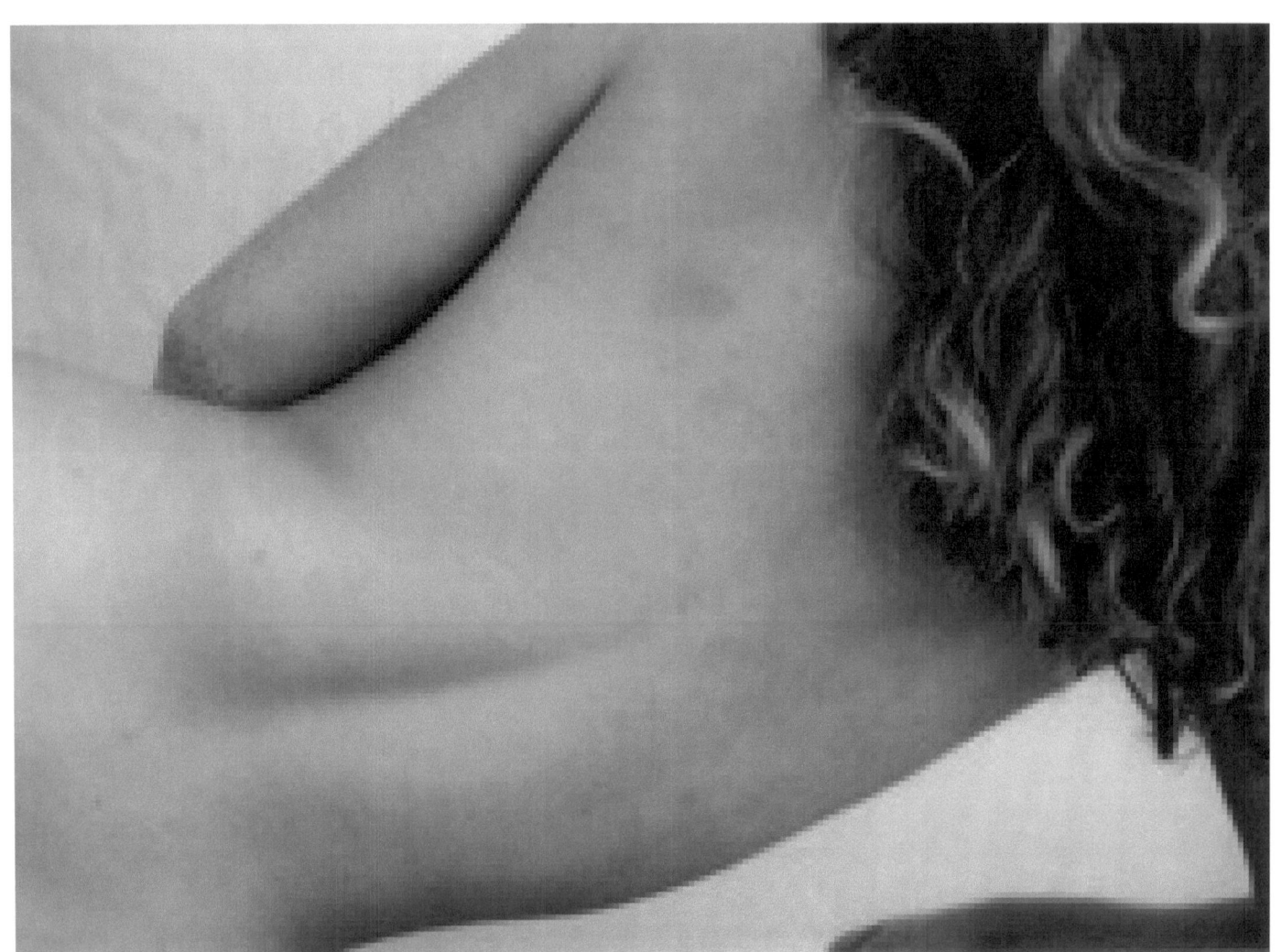

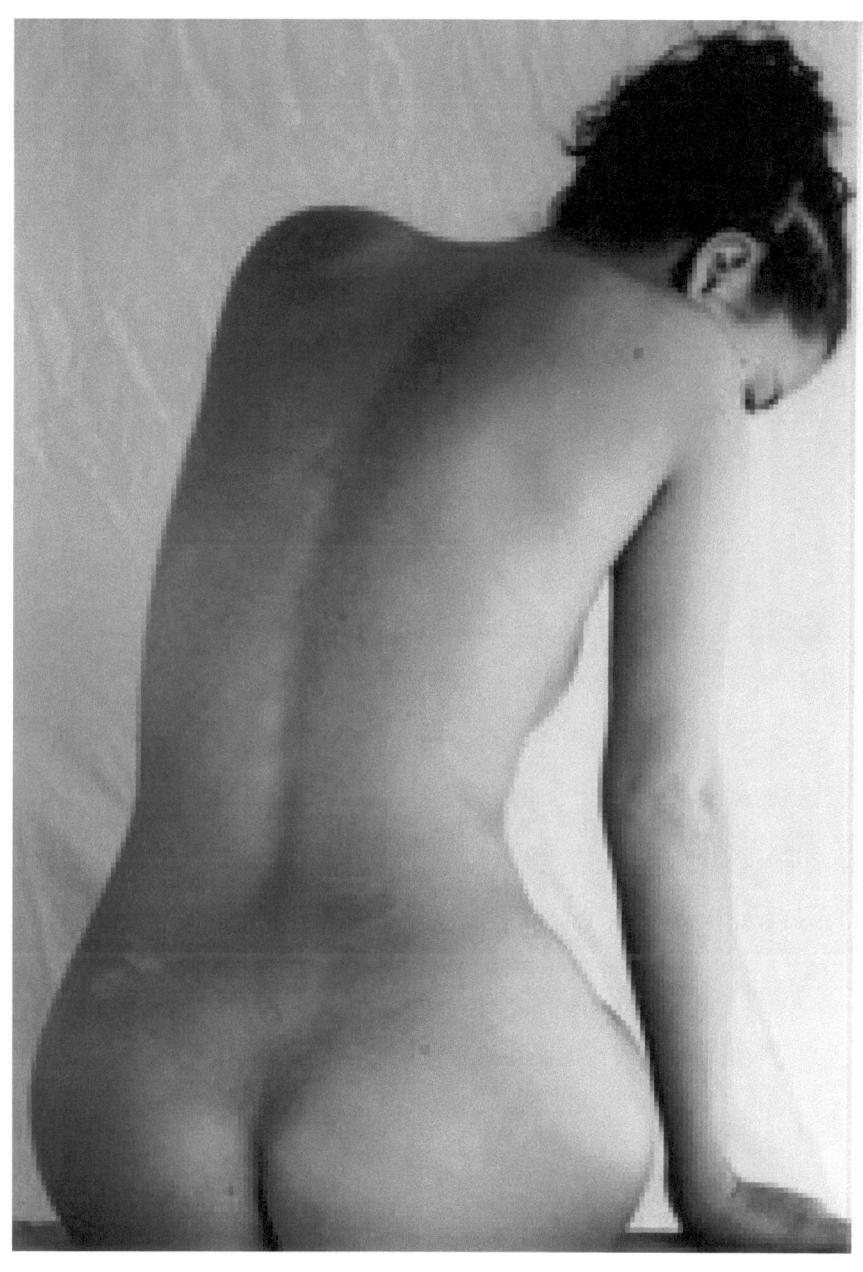

"Sitting Pretty" 2000

All nudes were shot at my apartment out on a south-facing balcony. I put up linen to defuse the sun and also to ensure privacy. Hence these photos were all shot using natural light.

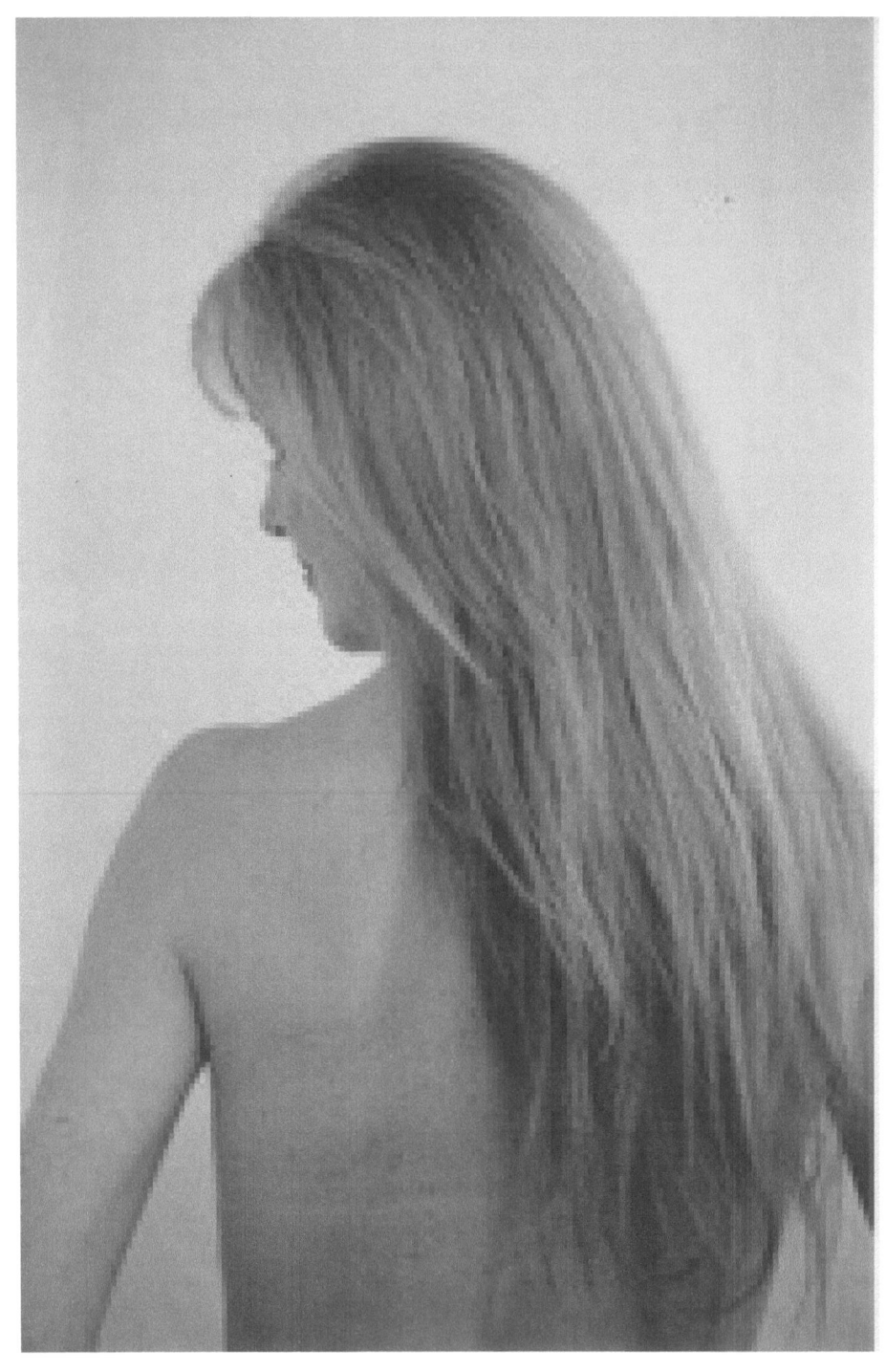

One of the sexier aspects I find of a woman is her hair. I have an affinity for long hair as it can play an intricate role in nude photography.

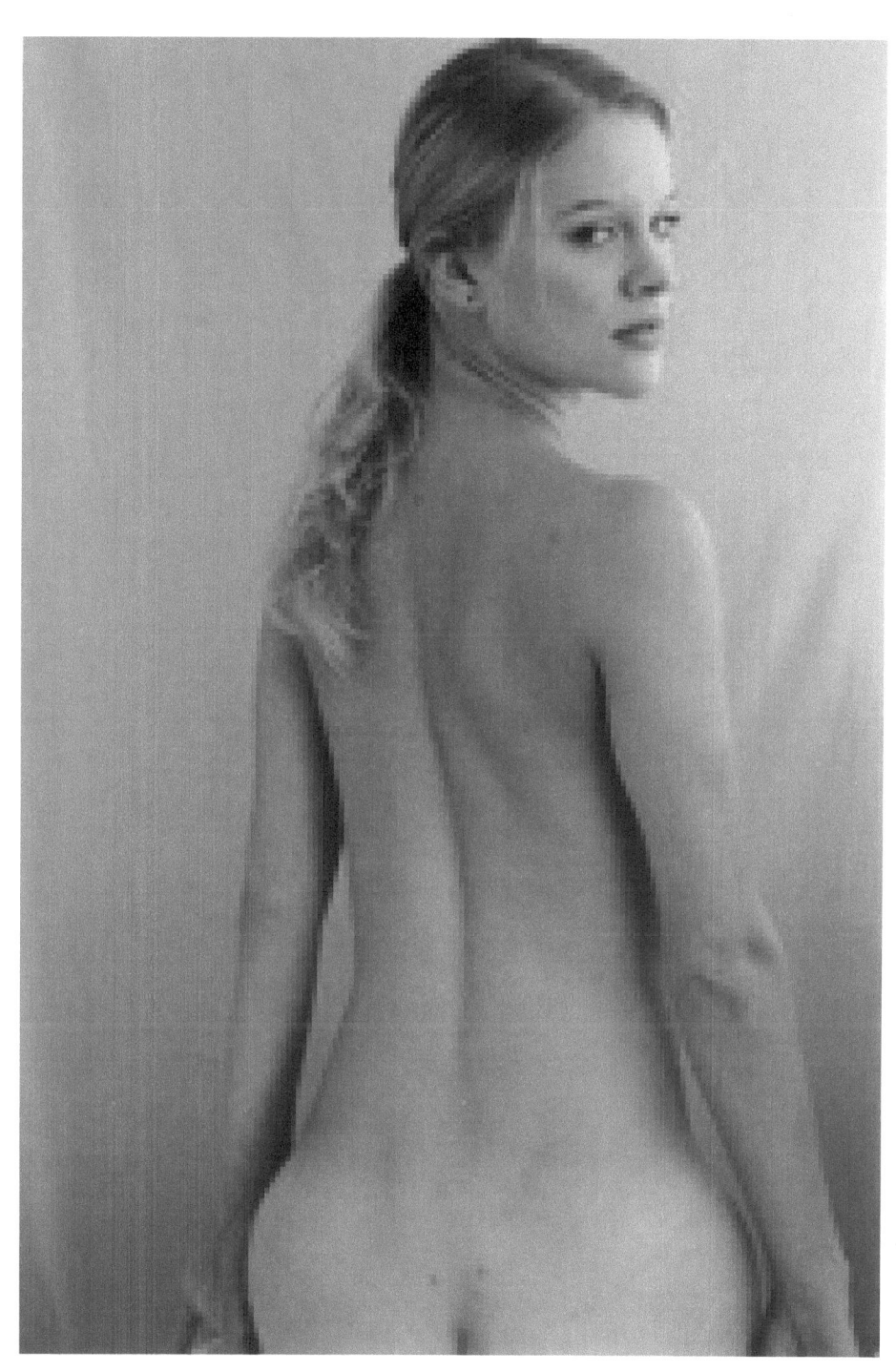

"Looking Back" 2000

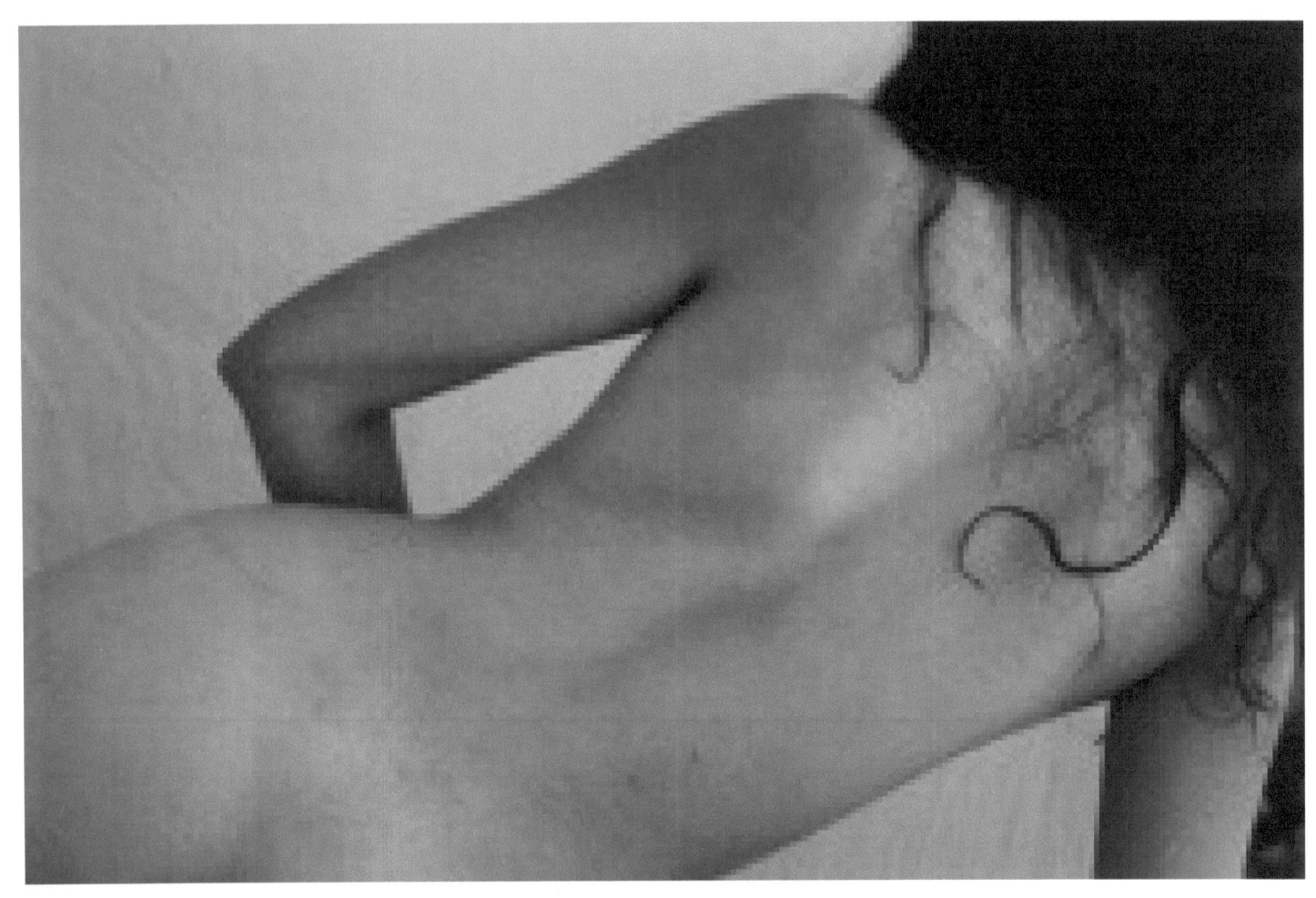

"Sideways" 2000

One of the more curvaceous places on a woman is her breasts, however, when shooting this area I was careful not to include the nipple, once again treading that fine line between art and perceived pornography.

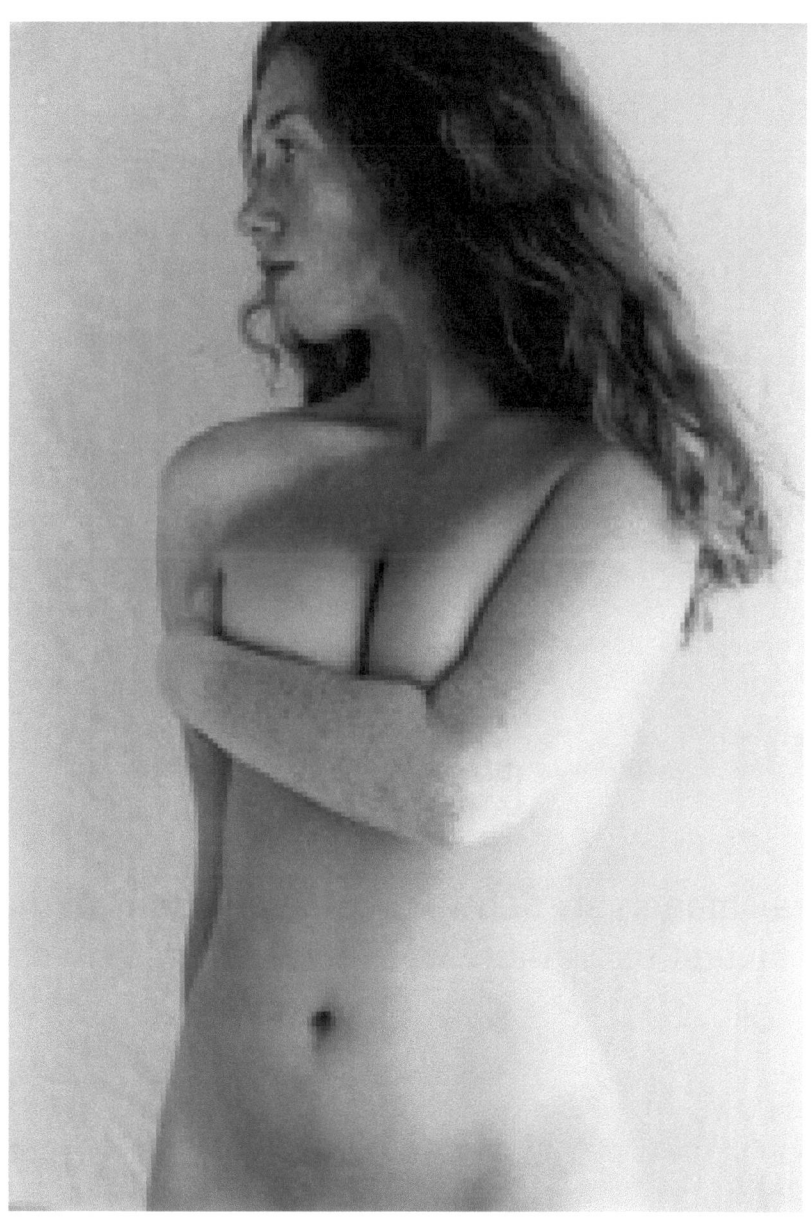

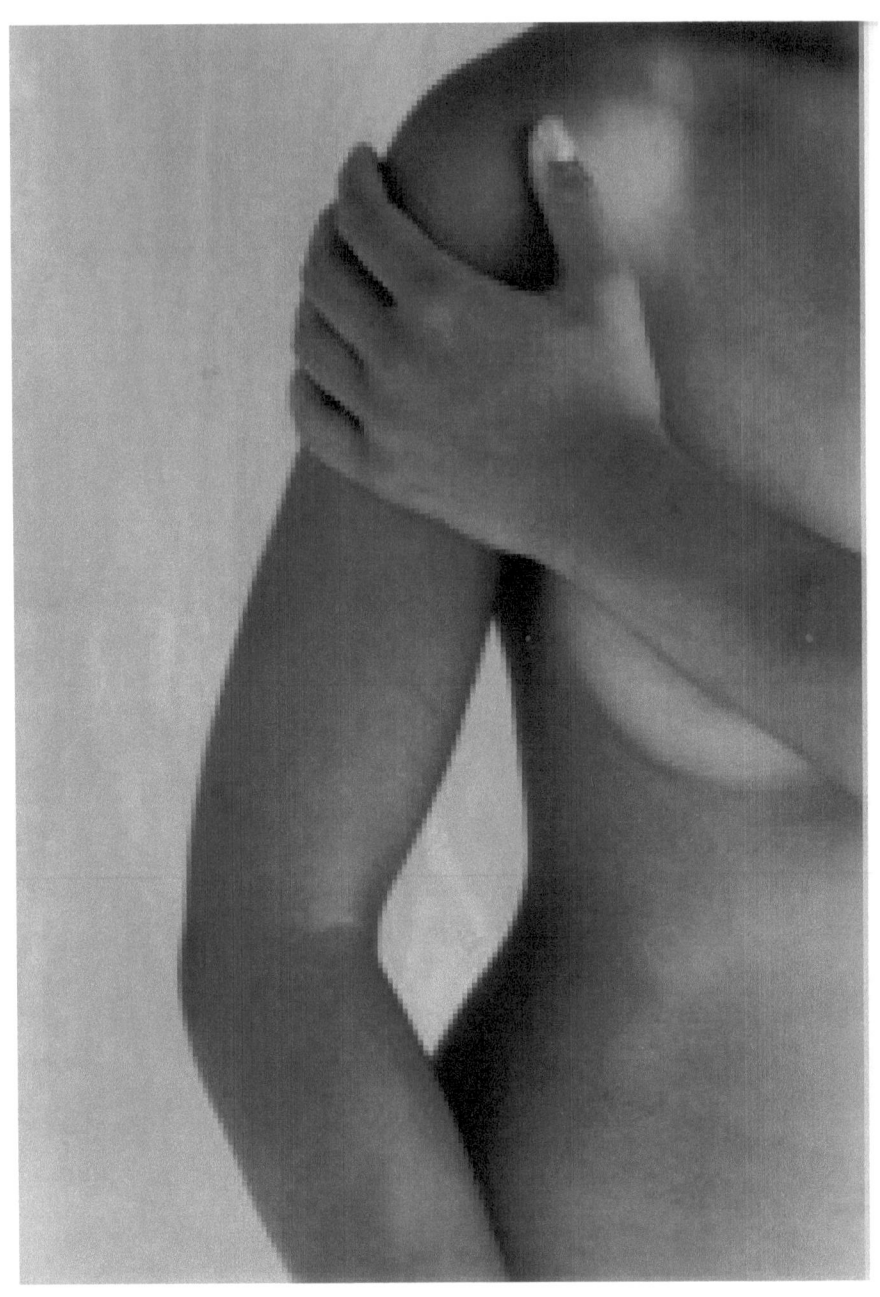

You'll notice that all models are subtly covering portions of themselves, as I didn't want to be blatant put rather suggestive in my discovery of the feminine form.

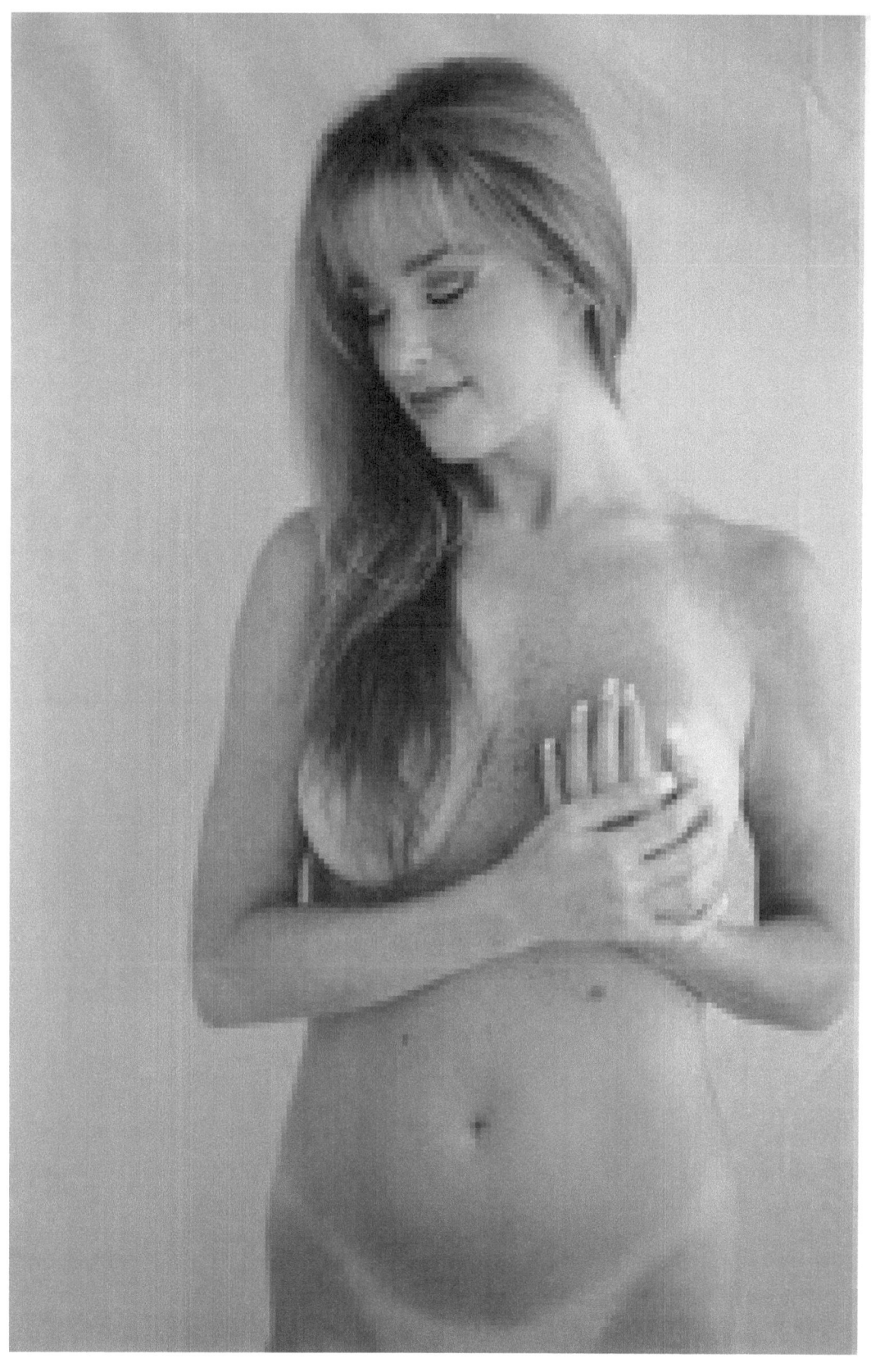

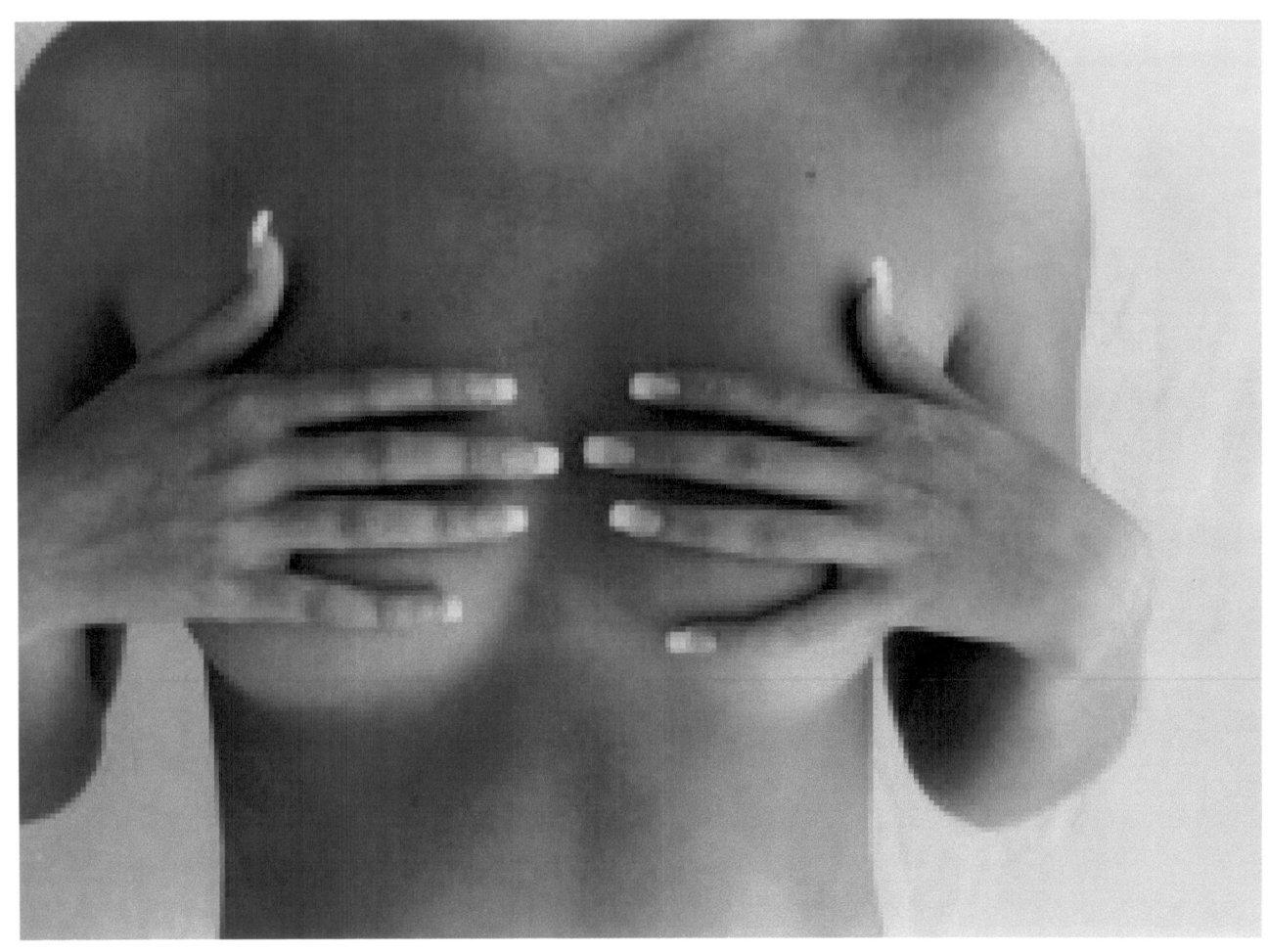

The delicacy of her hands covering her breasts, the subtle difference between art and pornography.
The success of taking nudes was to make the models feel relaxed and beautiful. They could quit anytime they wanted to though each session lasted only 20 – 40 minutes depending on what I needed and the models desired, as a part of their compensation was copies of their photographs.

I also had the opportunity to experiment with the female body and take some shots in various poses; including one who was with child, as seen below.

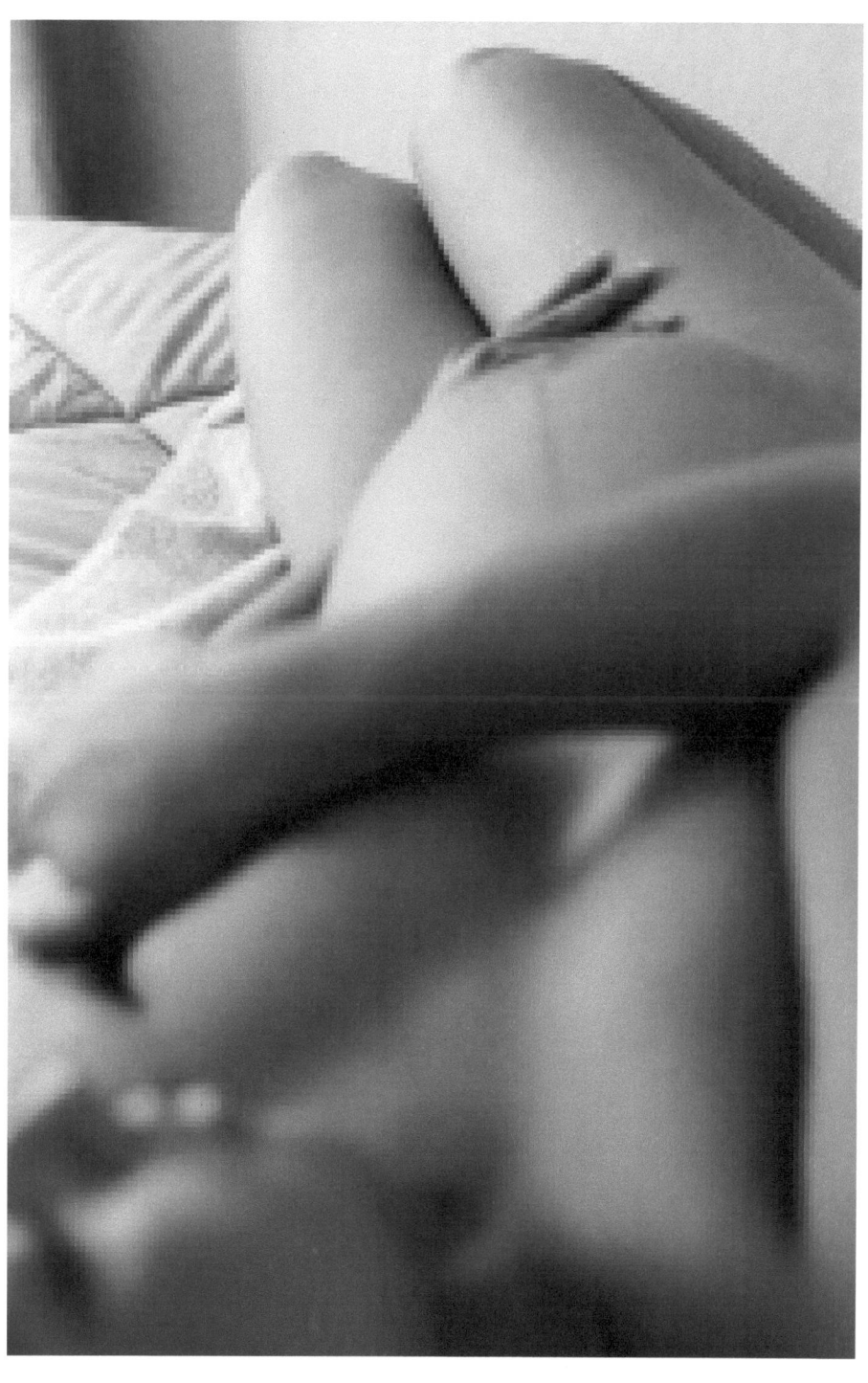

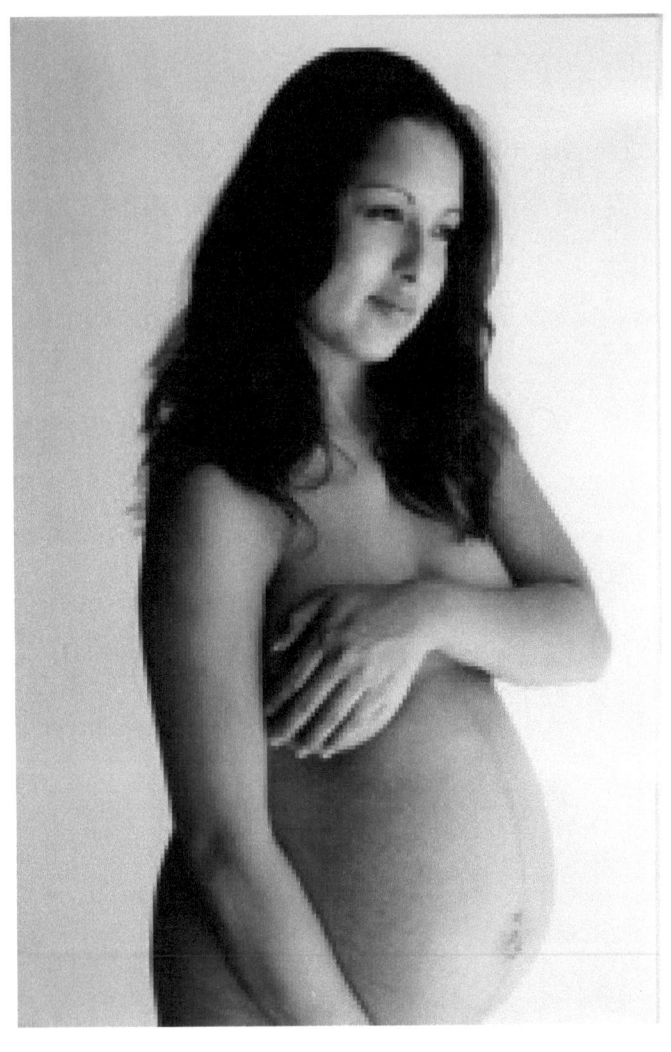

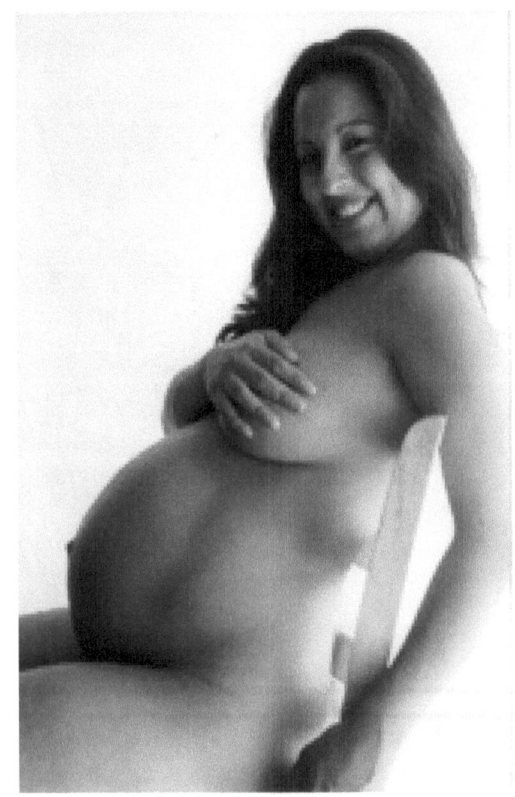

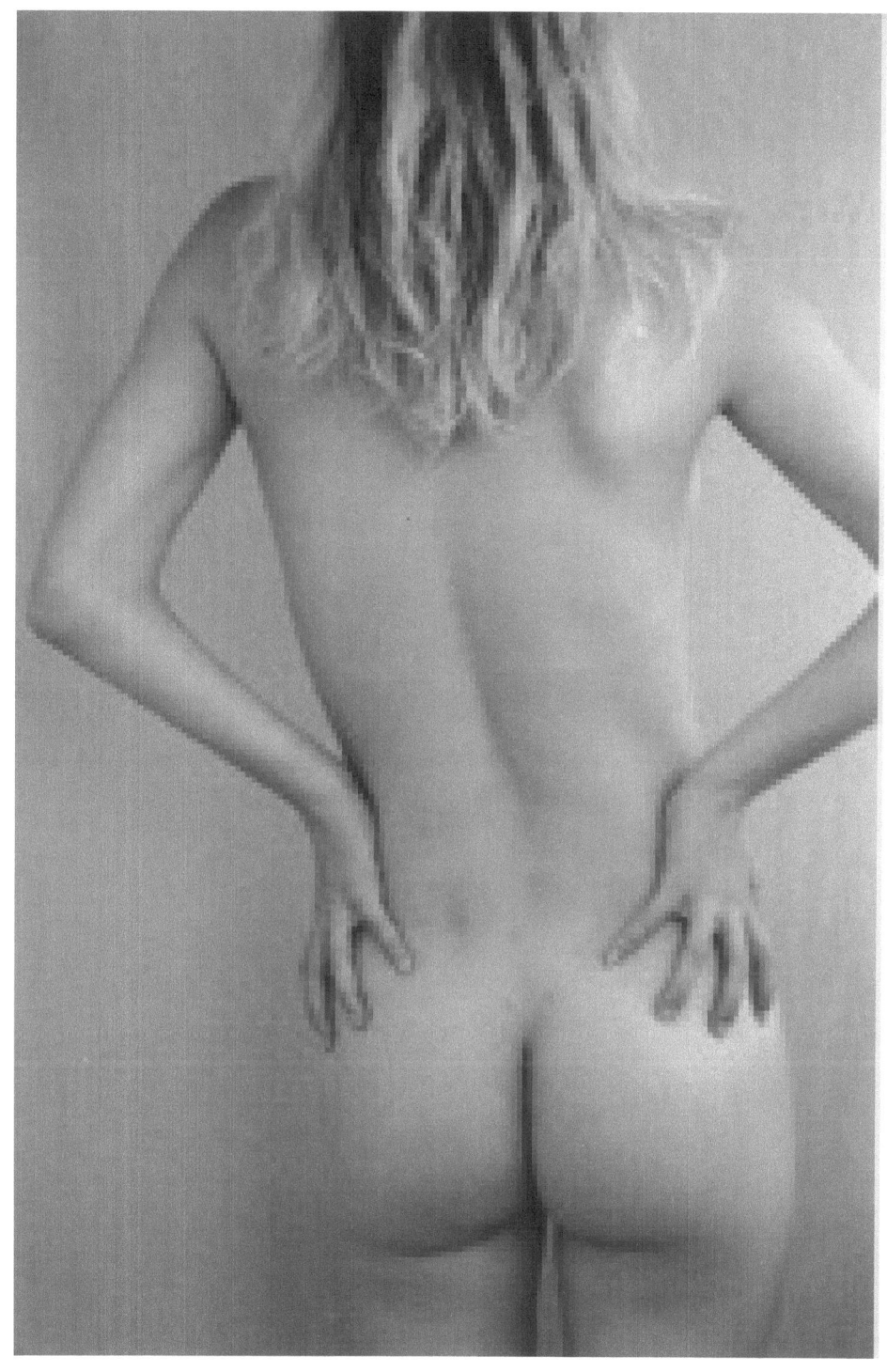

Take care in what or how you name your photos, for that name is liable to stick forever. If you can't come up with one, then choose a generic one. This one, for example is simply named "Hands on hips."

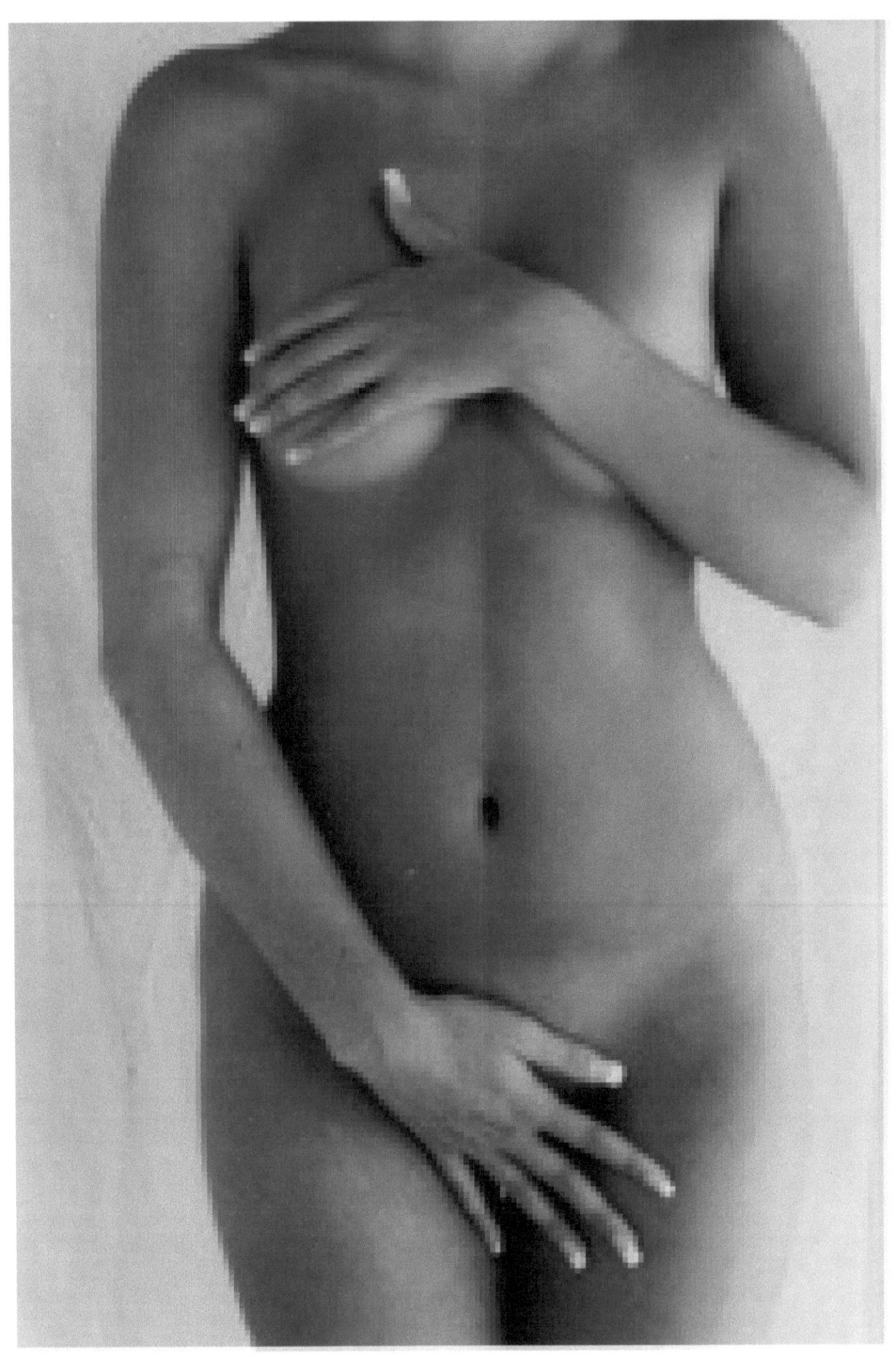

"Shy" 2000

I allowed the models to decide their own comfort levels and if they wish to remain anonymous. Therefore some pics are depicted decapitated which, fortunately, does not take away from the beauty of the photograph or the model.

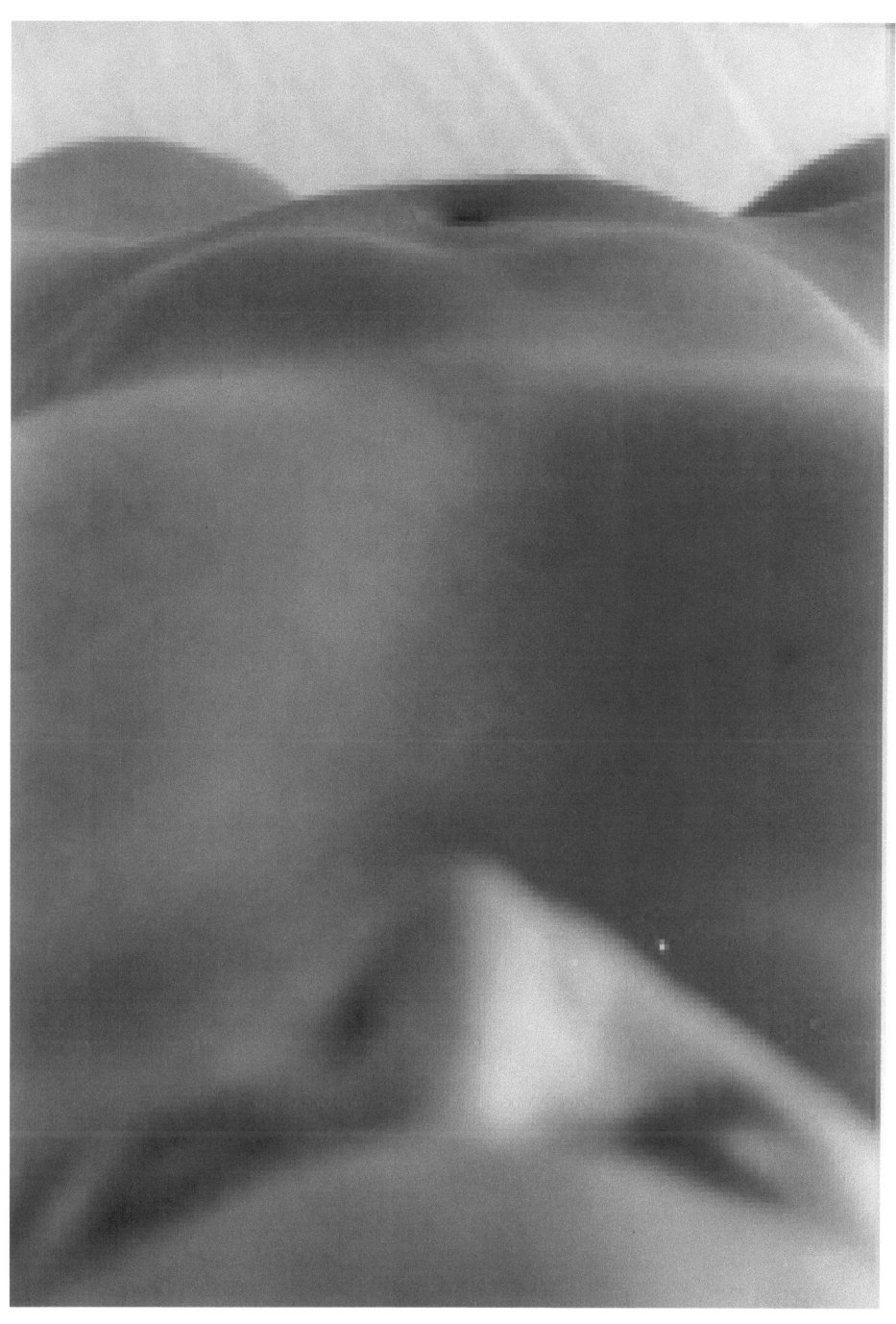

"Hills and Valleys" 2000

Trying different angles with models can be interesting and rewarding. You'll notice on all my nude shots that certain areas are not exposed. I did that purposely for my objective was the curves and angles of a woman's body and to take away any suspicions from fanatics that this may be pornography.

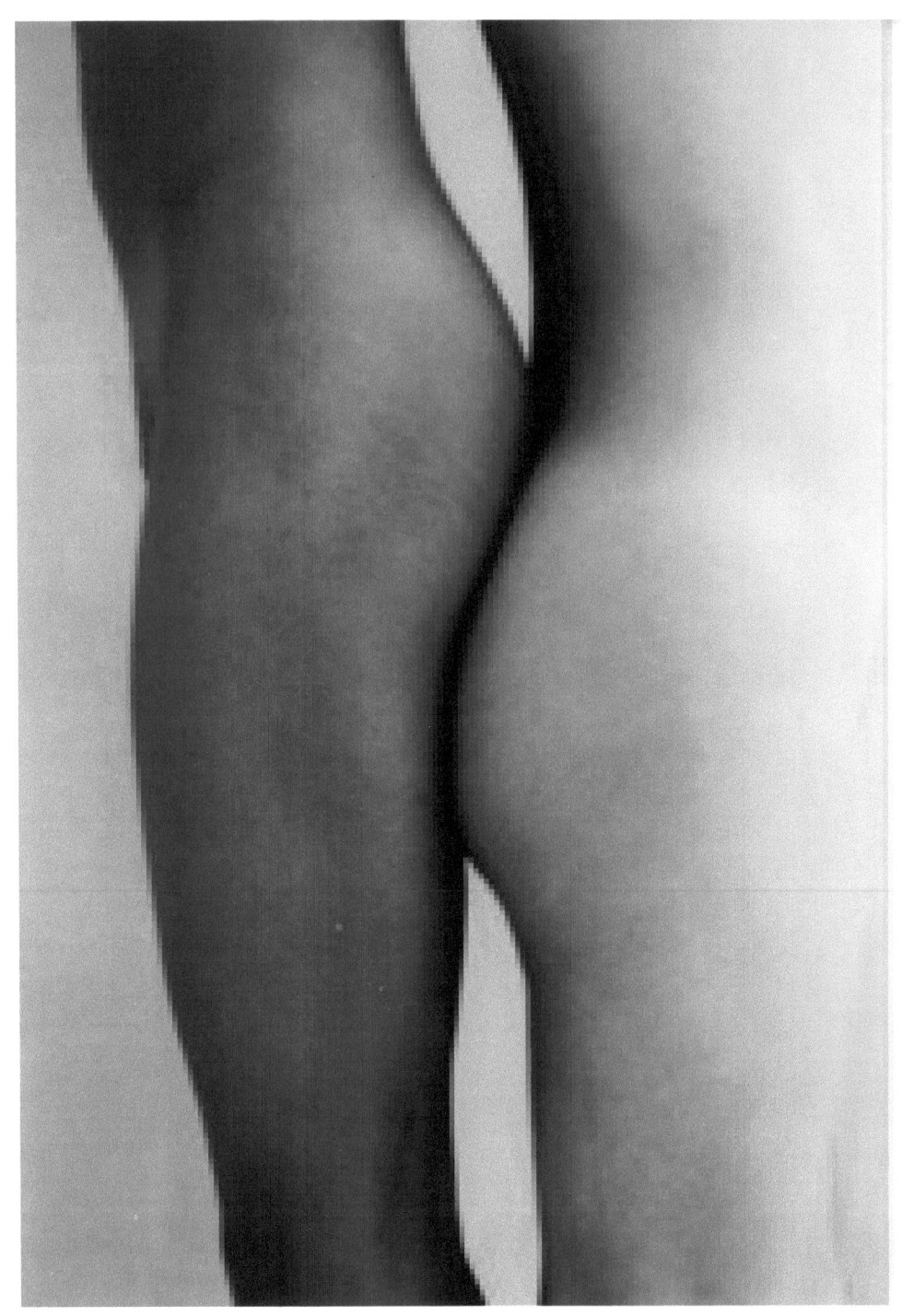

"Cheek to cheek" 2000

Working with two models produced this interesting photo. They came together and being friends there were no concerns to going back to back for this shot. The height difference between the two made the photo a natural.

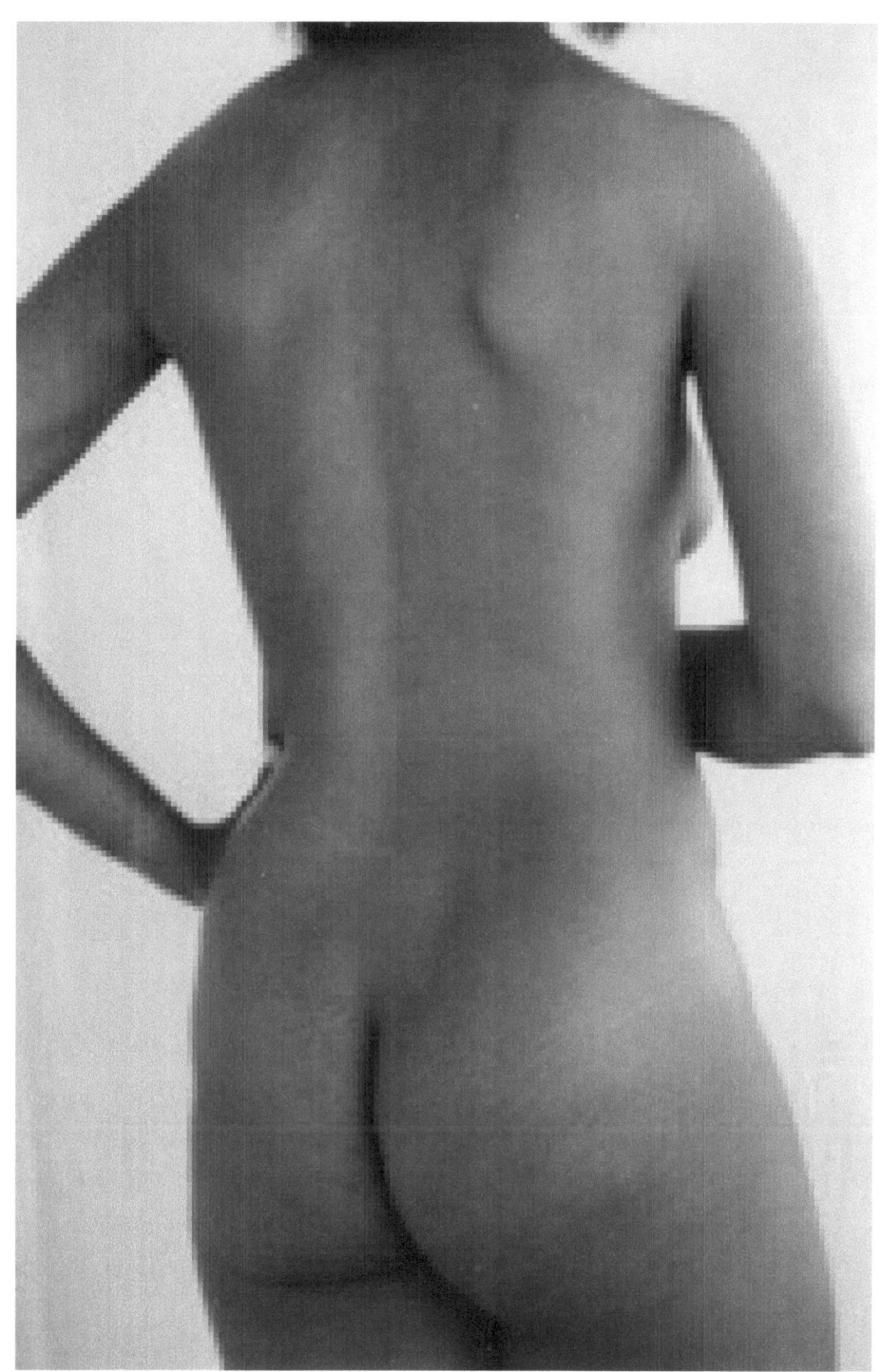

"Hand on hip" 2000

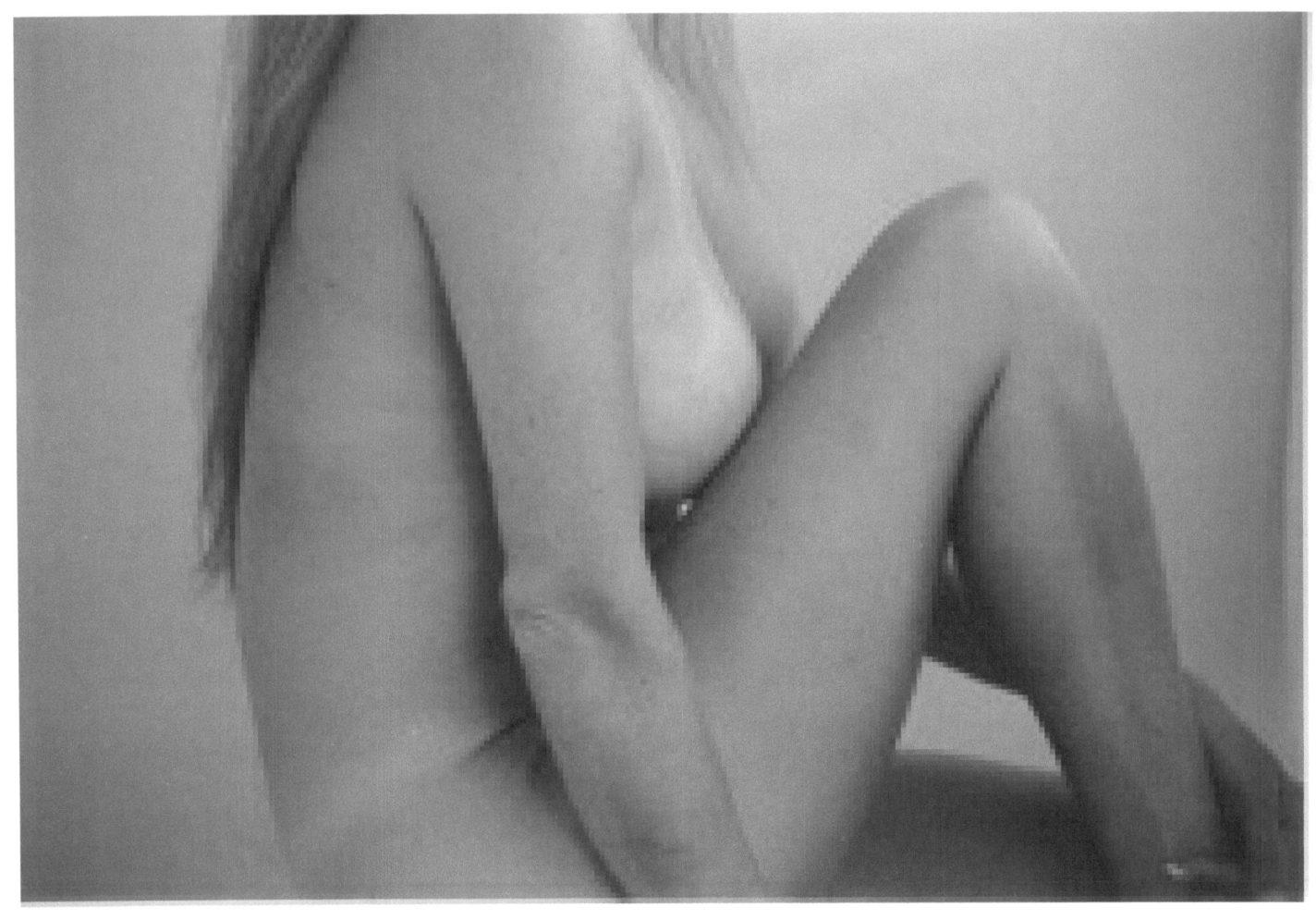

"Temptation" 2000

One important thing to remember when working with nudes is to keep things professional. You must strive to make your models comfortable, trusting and confident that the pics are used with the best intent as art. Any indication of questionable behavior and comments on your part cannot only ruin your career and reputation, but may bring legal action. So be careful when working with this genre.

It is easy wanting to shoot the young and beautiful, but there is a beauty that comes with maturity. Older women are usually more confident and graceful, but can be hesitant when posing nude. However, if the photos are done in good taste, you will find it a pleasure to work with them.

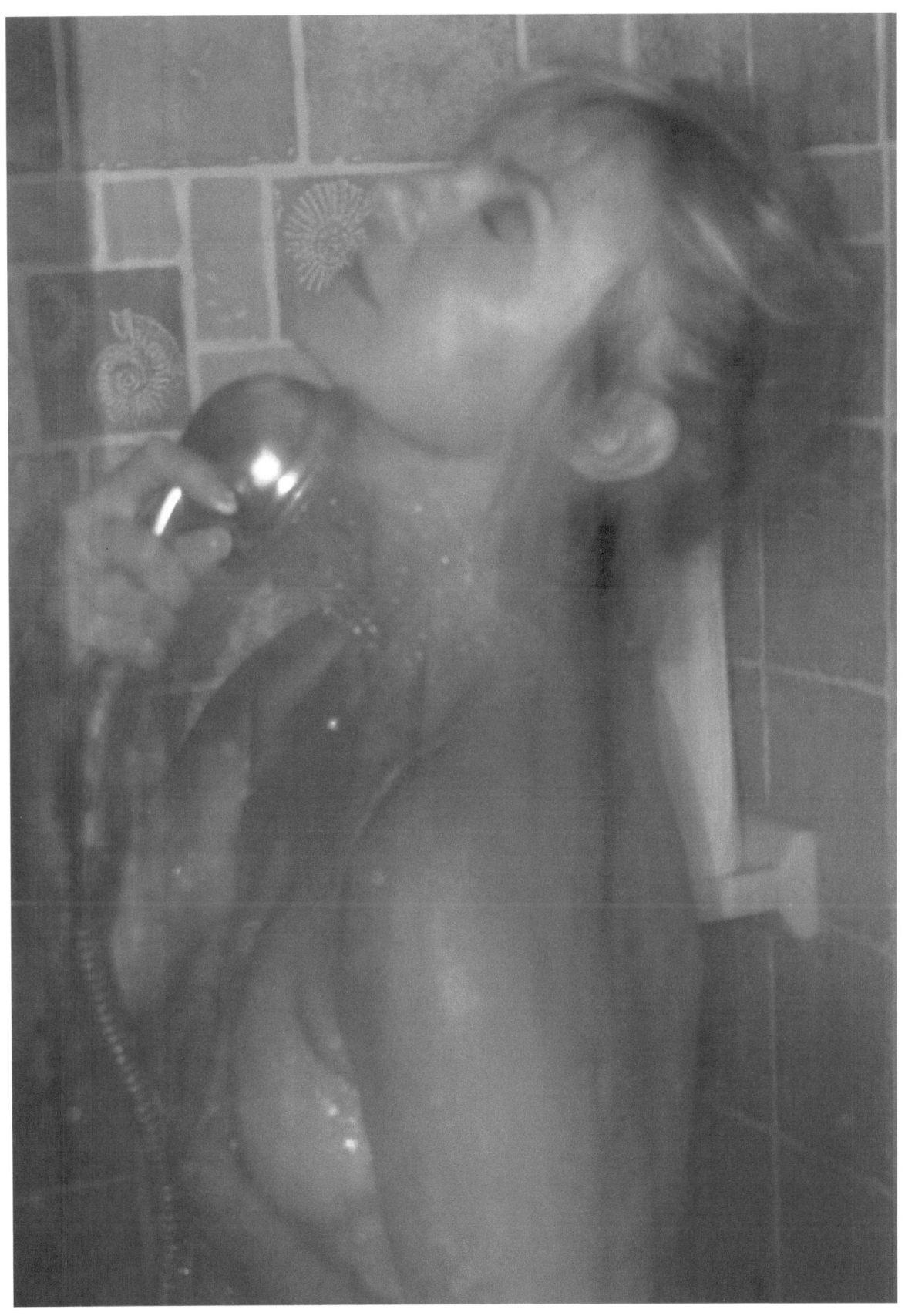

"The Shower" 2009

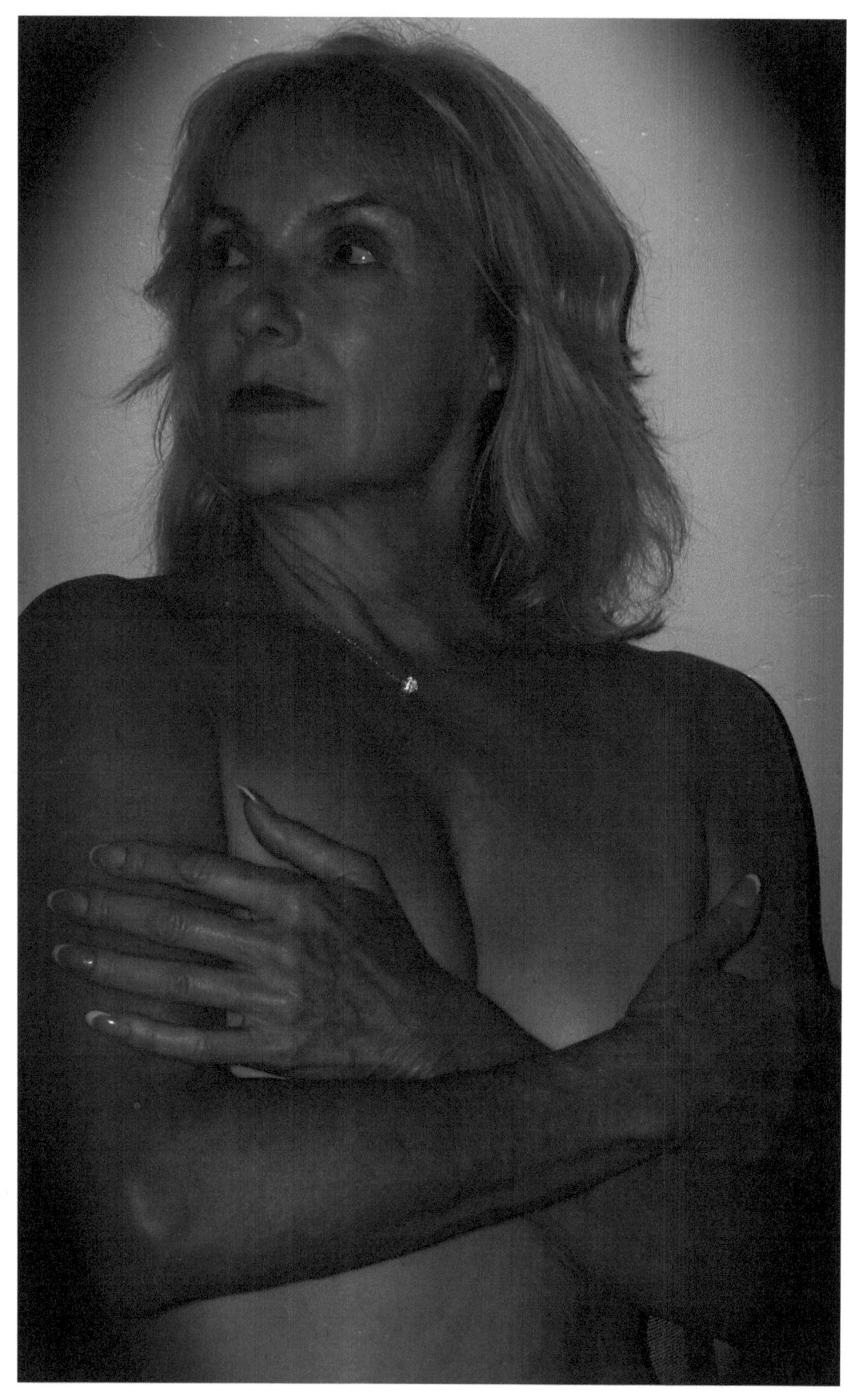

"Strength" 2009

Creating

Themes

Sometimes the best way to present your photos is through a theme. For instance, you shot a lot of flowers so you put them all together to create a "flower garden."

Now, what I mean by putting them together is presenting them on the same wall but as individual pieces. Placing them on the same print might make it look cluttered to your customers.

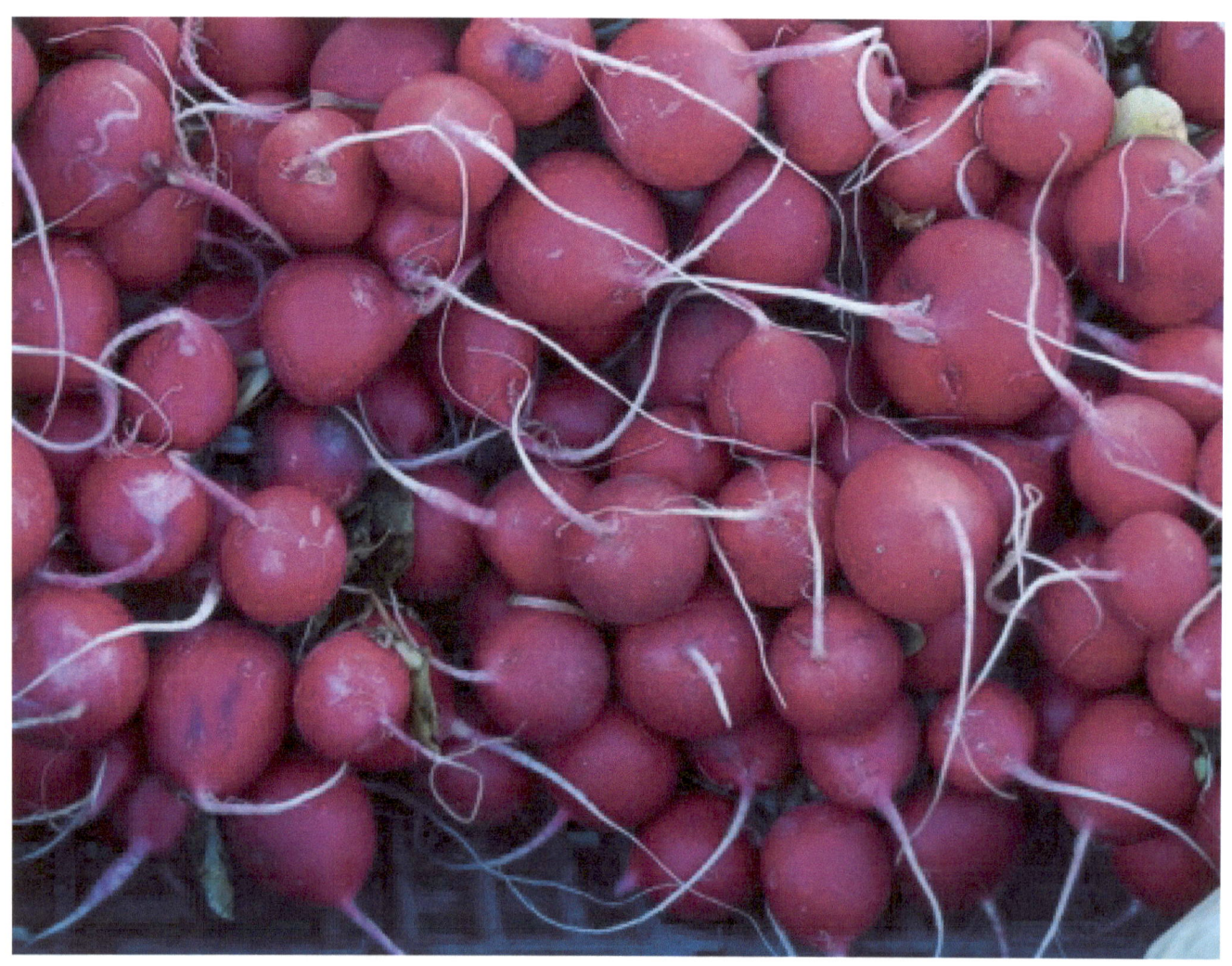

Radishes – Farmer's Market, Mesa, AZ 2009

Who would think to shoot fruits and veggies at a Farmer's Market? I would. It makes for great composition and color and keeps one's eye in a state of development. Besides, who says fruits and veggies don't take good pics? I used to shoot portraits.

Here are more pics? Why more? Fruits and veggies are good for you.

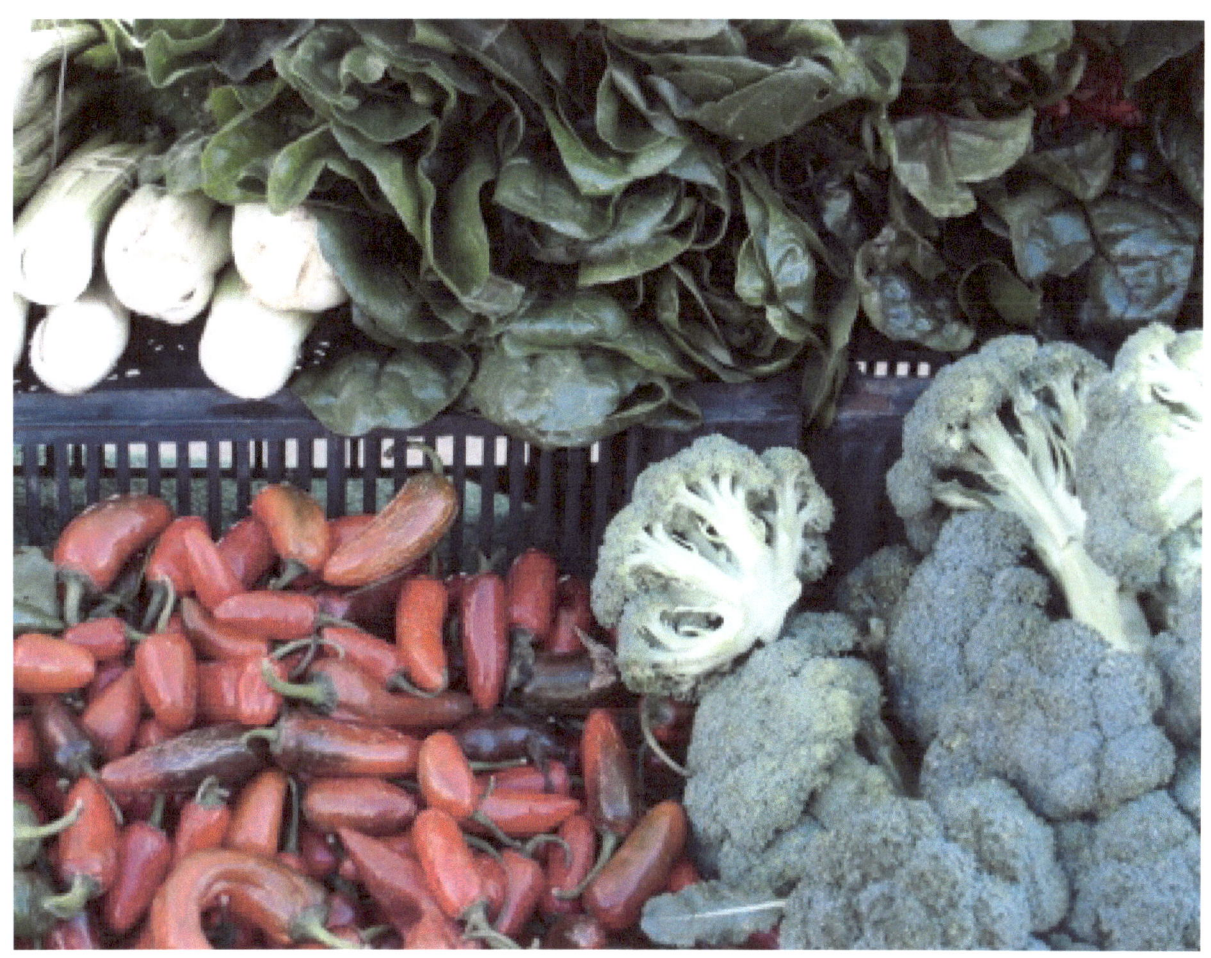

Aside from the colors, you'll notice the textures. In person it was also the smells and tastes that make Farmer's Markets a special place to visit.

In 2011 I produced a show called "Mood Food" out of Scottsdale. Once the food was prepared we had a panel of "food experts" taste the meal and comment on the mood food sets based on color, texture, smell and taste.

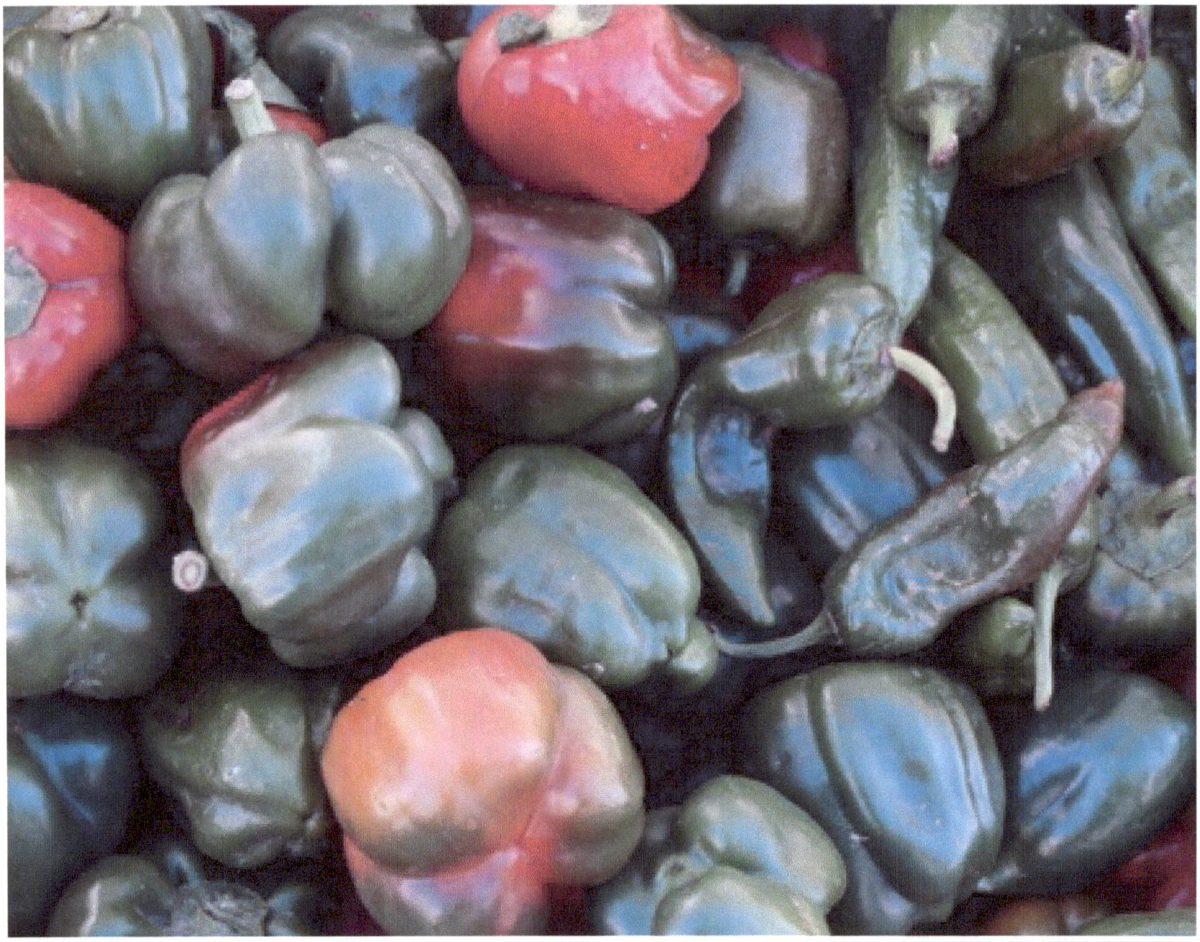

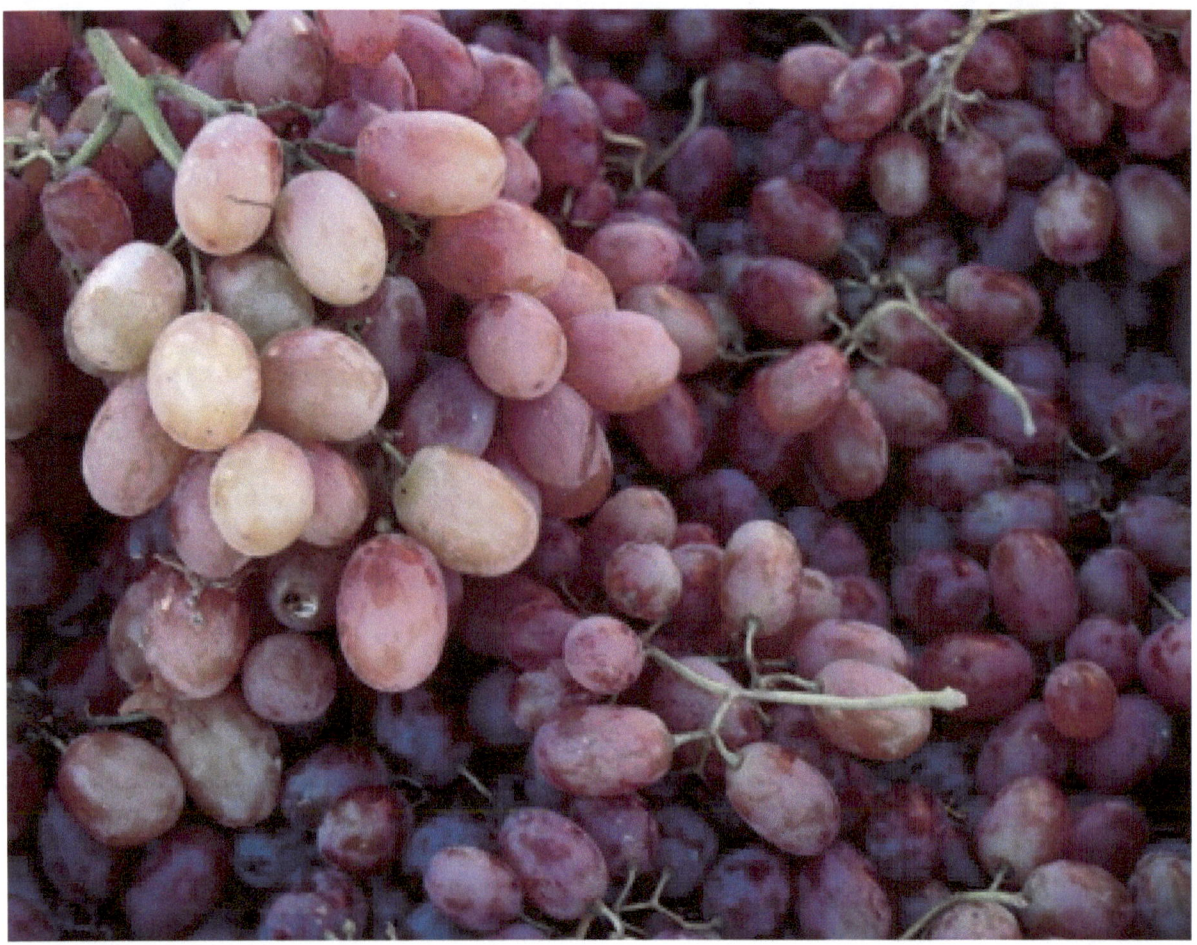

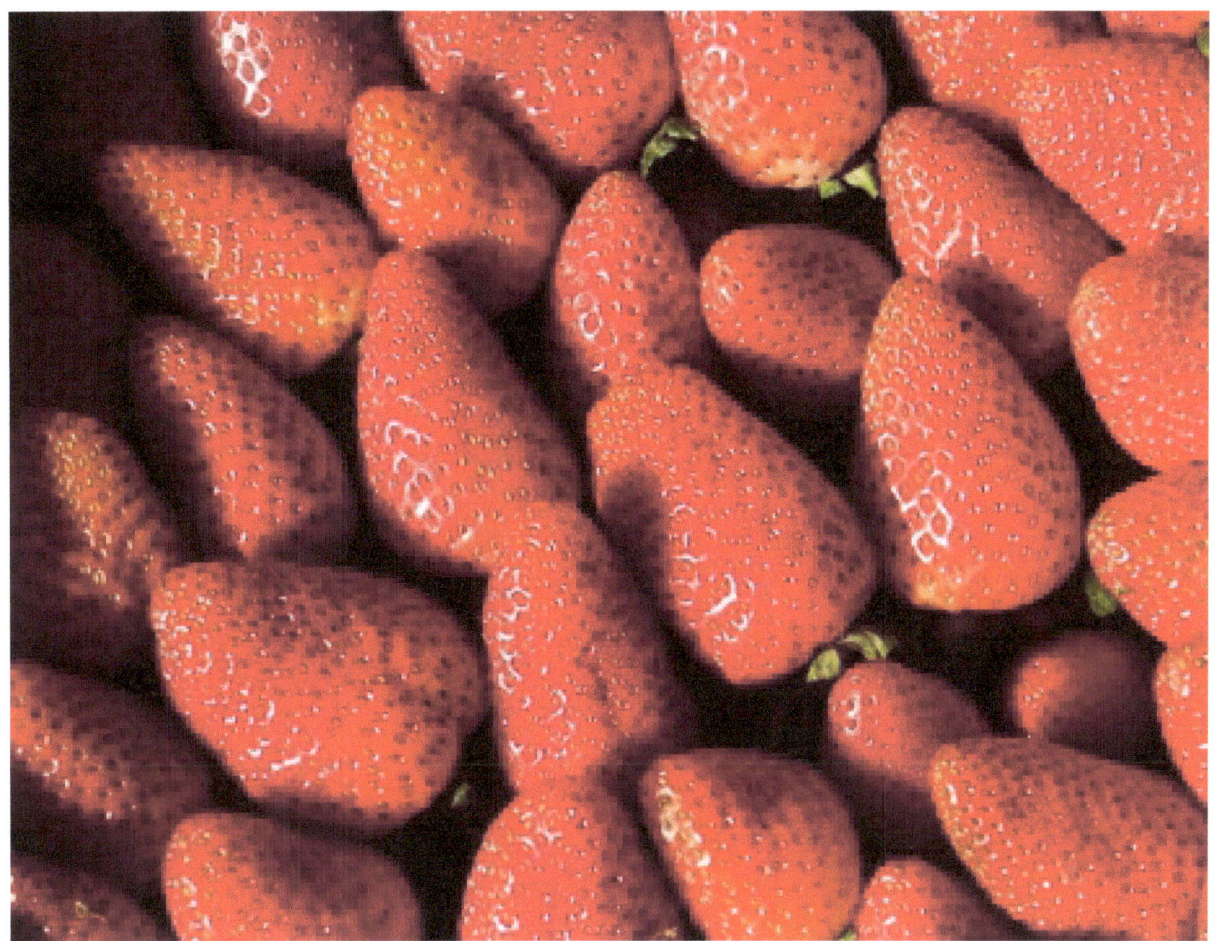

Shoot flowers as a theme has its drawbacks and rewards. Too many can look cluttered and take away from the intent. Focusing on one can make the viewer take note of what they've been missing by not examining the color and texture of a flower.

It's not just "Stop and smell the flowers," but see and take note of them too.

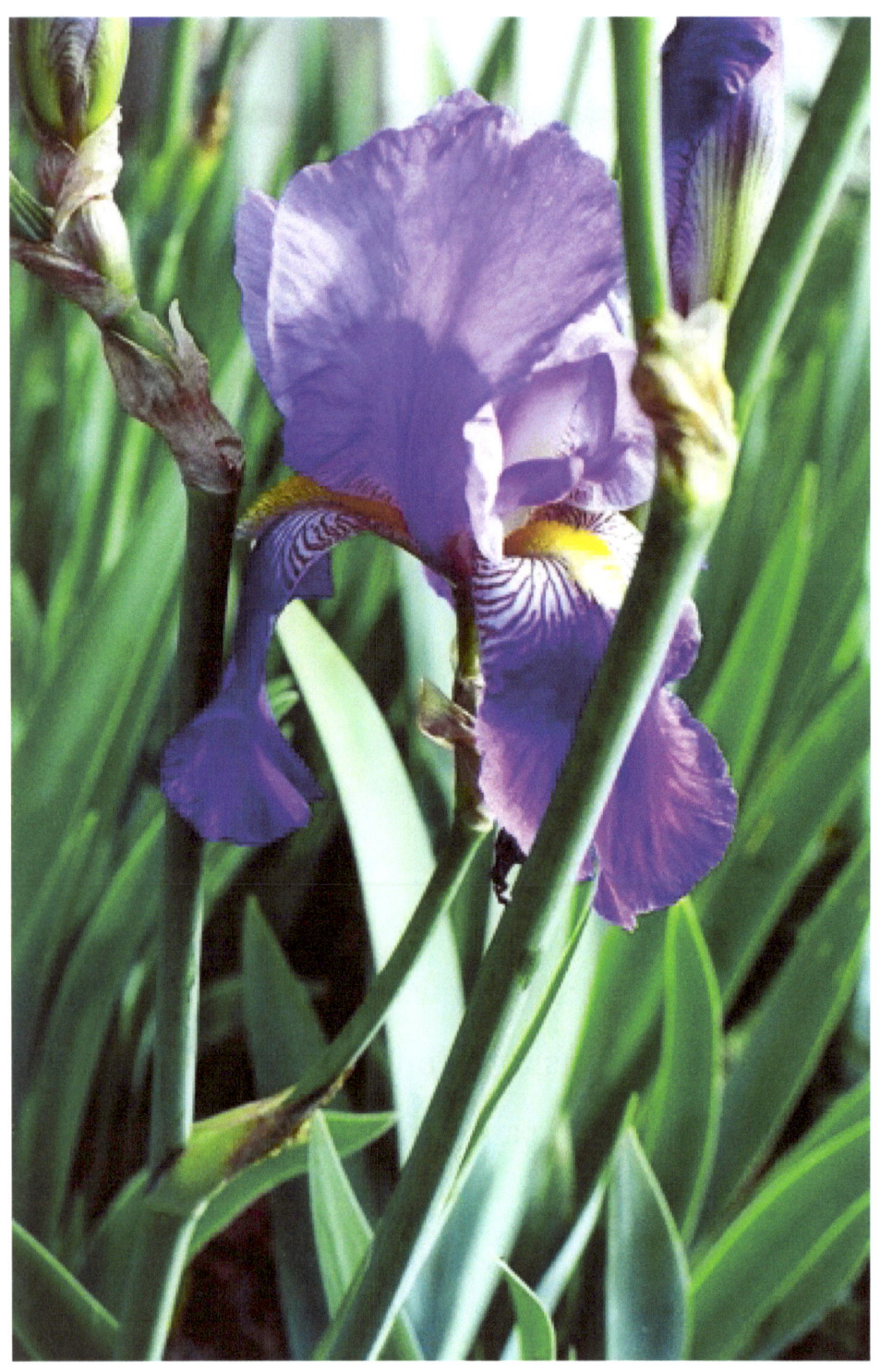

Iris – Time and place unknown

Flowers are fleeting as well. When you see a beautiful bouquet as put out by Mother Nature, don't hesitate to shoot it.

Flora and Fauna may not interest you right now, but take my word, there is an audience for them and having a good stock of photos on this subject will only increase your chances of sales in the future.

Besides that, anytime you can develop your skills as a photographer by taking pictures of things that you normally wouldn't shoot is a good learning experience and keeps your eye sharp.

The Flower Garden

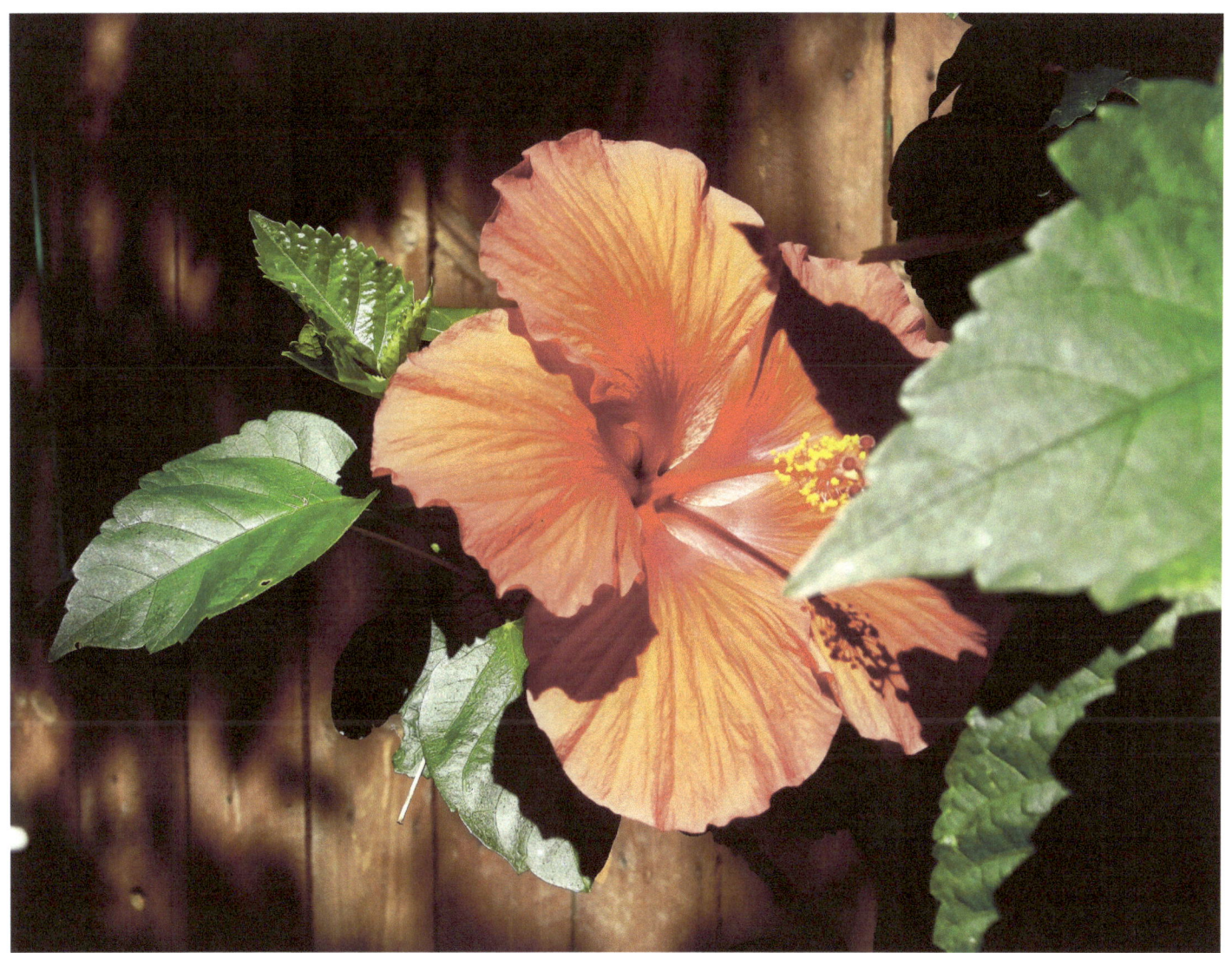

When shooting outside be aware of the natural lighting and shadows; they can be a blessing or a burden. As you look at the subject via window or eyepiece, check out the entire picture within the frame before shooting.

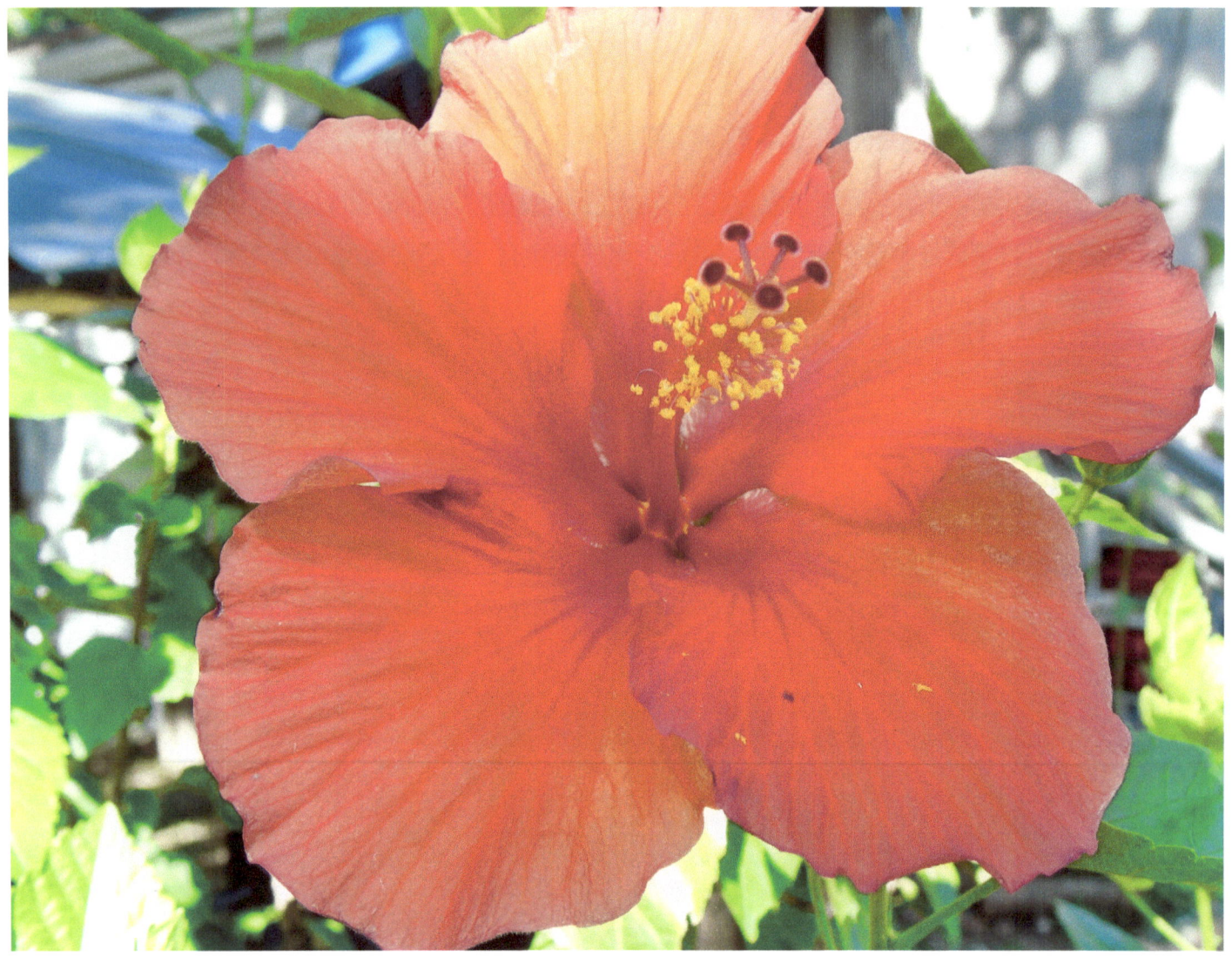

Hibiscus   2017

Focus on the flower's prominent feature. Is it the coloration, design, or the stamen? This should take center stage.

When going for multiple flowers, as in a garden, be sure they bunch nicely and there aren't a lot of dead ones that might interfere with the composition you're trying to create.

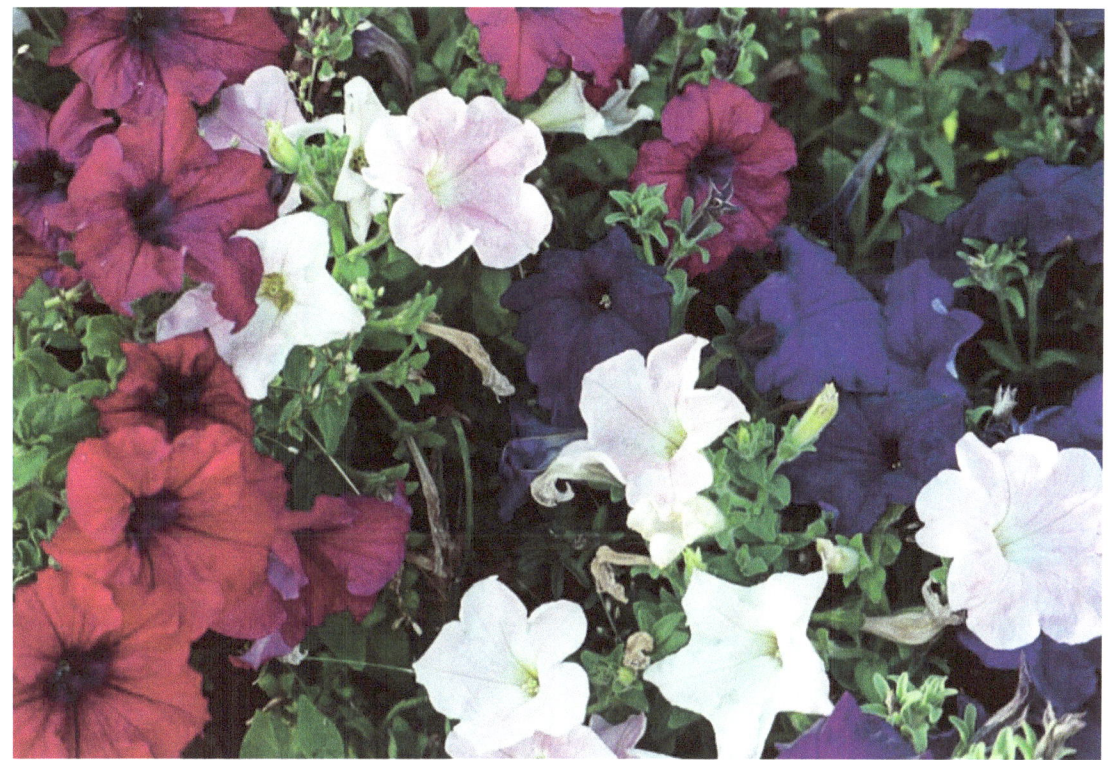

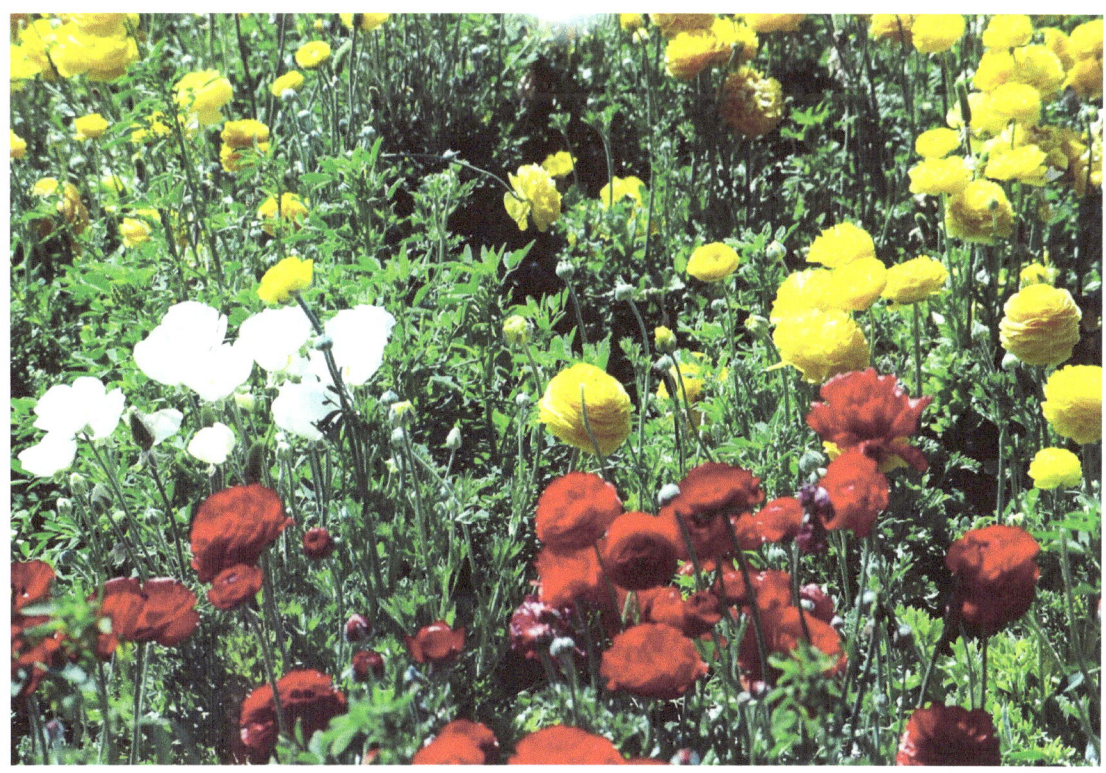

Sharpening the image to the fore ground can leave a nice blurred effect behind, especially if it's the same plant.

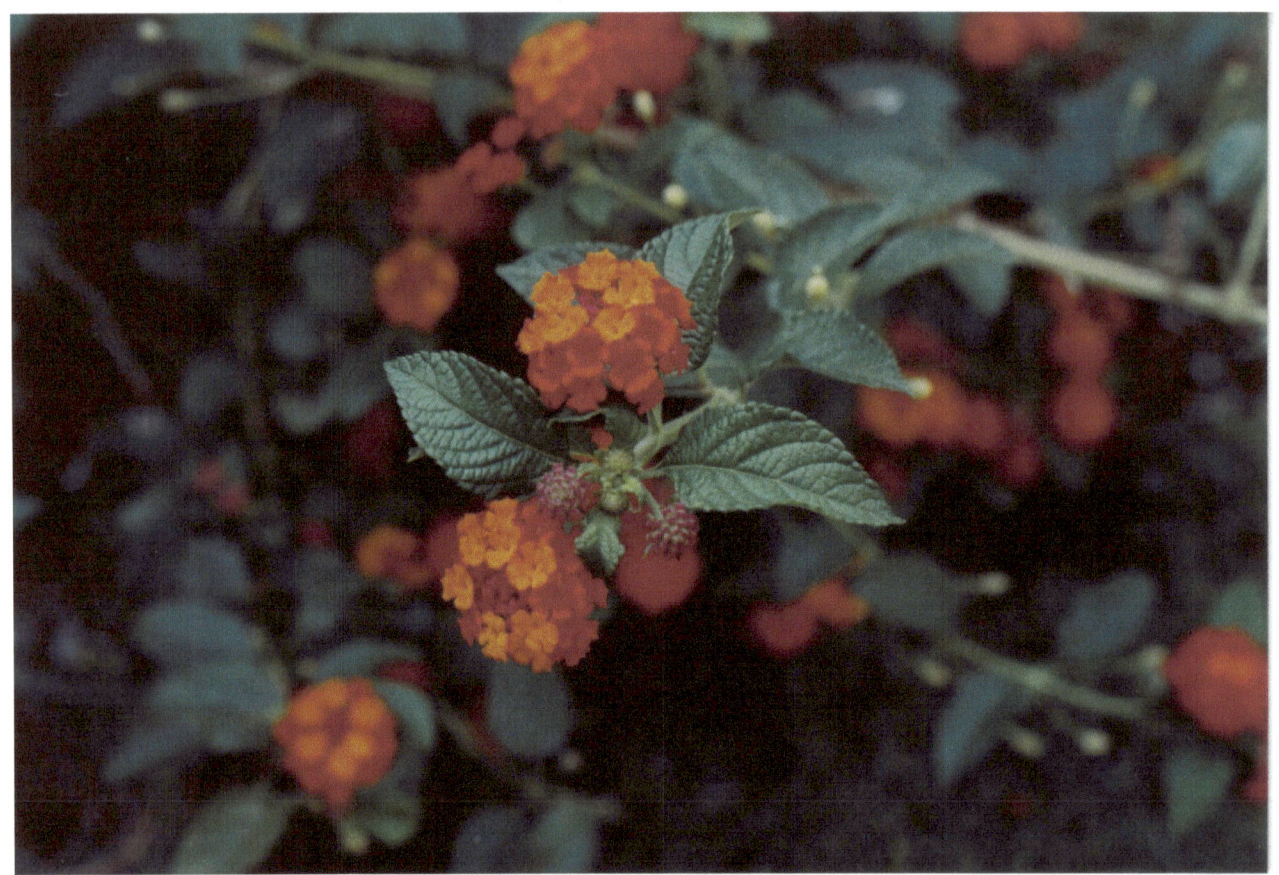

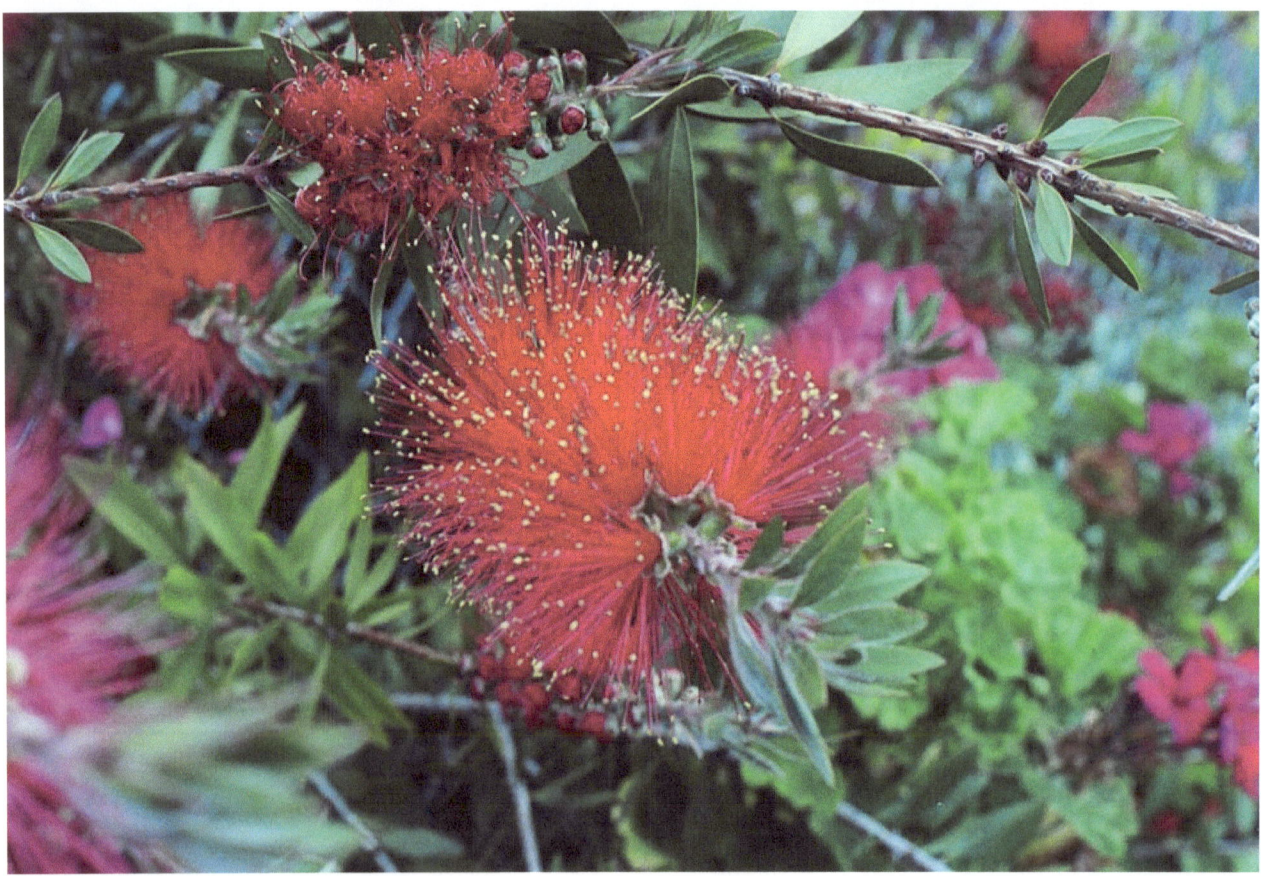

I've

Been

Framed

And Matted

Matting and framing can be as crucial to the success of your photographic art as the photo itself. When matting and framing my photography I look at the distinctive colors in the photograph and what color in particular I wish to exploit. That becomes the color of the matting.

Second is the type and color of the frame, which can add depth and warmth to a photo. Many photographic artists will keep matting and framing simple allowing their patrons to frame it as they wish. Others become extravagant making the frame the showpiece while the photograph gets lost in the frame. The trick is to be subtle while still making the photograph the center of attention, complementing it with the color and style of the matting and frame. Matting and framing your work can become the most expensive part in presenting your work. The best thing is to find frames at thrift stores, garage sales and sites such as Craig's List. Keep an eye out for galleries that may be disposing of frames or that are closing.

Taking pictures vs photography.

Anyone can take a picture. Almost every cell phone has photo capabilities and people take a boatload of pics on everything imaginable and some not so imaginable. They take pics on their favorite subject, the selfie, and on subjects designed to hurt and criticize others. In other words they take pics for some of the wrong reasons, but also to document events and special occasions. This is NOT photography.

Photography is an art, a set of skills procured over a long period of time of trial and error, blood, sweat and tears with bouts of hysteria and laughter thrown in at the most peculiar and auspicious times. Photography is, in itself, an event and the photographer a self-editor at the moment the shot is being taken. True photographers know when to say "no," and when to open themselves up for the truly amazing.

There's nothing wrong with picture taking. It provides a visual journal of times and events in your life, but it doesn't mean you're a photographer. If you think you are, or want to be, take a few classes at your local community college so you can have your worked critiqued. This way you'll know if you should invest the time and money should you decide to go pro and sell your work. Professional photography is a commitment.

If you are interested in seeing more of my work, you may find it at the following sites.

Social Media and Websites

www.Facebook.com/tomashowephotography

www.viewbug.com/member/TomasHowe

Please send all inquiries to: tomashowephotography4u@gmail.com